The Boys From Grover Avenue

The Boys From Grover Avenue
Ed McBain's 87th Precinct Novels

George N. Dove

Bowling Green State University Popular Press
Bowling Green, OH 43403

Contents

Chapter 1

Crime-Detection on a Slanting Screen

The year 1956 was a particularly good time for starting a police series, because public taste at that point was running in favor of the police mystery. Television featured several shows with cop detectives, including especially the fabulous *Dragnet,* which had captured the public fancy as few broadcast series ever have. Eleven years earlier Lawrence Treat had published a mystery novel, *V as in Victim*, in which the detection was carried on by some capable but not especially brilliant policemen who employed the normal methods of real-life cops instead of the intellectual powers of a genius like Ellery Queen, and by 1956 Treat's novel had been expanded into a series of eight police stories.

The type of story Lawrence Treat wrote was a suspense tale in which the mystery was solved by a run-of-the-mill police detective named Mitch Taylor and a lab scientist named Jub Freeman. The procedures they used for detecting crime were much like those later employed by the popular Joe Friday and Frank Smith of *Dragnet,* consisting of stakeouts and tailings, questioning of witnesses and suspects, and most especially a strong reliance on the police laboratory. It was the employment of these routines that gave the new type its name, the police procedural. In these stories there is rarely a single detective "hero," the best results being achieved by policemen working in teams, as they do in non-fictional investigations. Far from evincing a narrative letdown, though, the police procedural was demonstrating that it could generate quite as much excitement and suspense as the mental exertions of the intellectual genius or the exotic gyrations of the hard-boiled private eye.

1

It was, indeed, a time of exciting innovation. In 1952 Hillary Waugh had published the police procedural *Last Seen Wearing...*, now considered one of the masterpieces of the mystery genre. In England in 1954 Maurice Procter had begun the Inspector Martineau series, and the following year saw the publication of *Gideon's Day,* by John Creasey using the pseudonym J. J. Marric, the beginning of what was to become another classic procedural series. Thus, the appearance in 1956 of a paperback entitled *Cop Hater* by Ed McBain provided additional stimulus to the public appetite for police procedural stories, more especially so when it was followed up by *The Mugger* and *The Pusher* during the same year.

It was the sharp eye of Anthony Boucher, then mystery critic of the *New York Times,* that spotted these three little Permabook editions as distinguished contributions to the procedural school, and he included *Cop Hater* and *The Mugger* in his list of Best Suspense Novels of 1956.[1] When the first three stories were collected into a hardback volume for publication by Simon and Schuster in 1959, Boucher wrote an introduction which contained one especially insightful judgment:

> ...McBain's performance was something possibly even more valuable than invention: at exactly the right historical moment he managed to write, with more striking effect than anyone before him, what readers were hungering for with already whetted appetites.[2]

At the end of this introduction Boucher identified McBain as Evan Hunter, already well known to the reading public as the author of *The Blackboard Jungle, Strangers When We Meet,* and several others, some written under his own name and others under the pseudonym Richard Marsten.

As Boucher recognized, there was little in these first 87th Precinct stories to distinguish them from other police procedurals, except that they were much better written than most. When we re-read them now, we may be struck by the absence of those qualities that have come to distinguish the 87th Precinct stories, and to be impressed by the similarity of their tone to that of the more conventional cop story. The changes that have been worked into the series are the marks of Ed McBain's maturing style.

It would appear that McBain's intention in the early stories was to write straight "realistic" crime fiction. One of the realities of police work, for example, is that policemen are frequently killed on the job; consequently, three policemen die in *Cop Hater* and another is seriously wounded. We know now that Steve Carella was scheduled to be killed in *The Pusher,* but even that early he had become such a popular favorite that McBain's editor would not permit his death,[3] and since that time the number of police deaths in the 87th Precinct has been gratifyingly small, marking a decided departure from the dictates of "realism."

Another early change of direction resulted in the introduction of the fantastic pair of homicide detectives, Monoghan and Monroe, who now constitute one of the trademarks of the series. There are a couple of homicide dicks on the scene early in *Cop Hater*, an un-named pair who exchange the conventional rough cop banter with Carella and Bush, but they are largely undistinguished from the general run of hard-spoken city detectives in police fiction. Monoghan and Monroe show up in *The Mugger,* still engaging in the tough conversation-out-of-the-side-of-the-mouth of their predecessors, but something else begins to get into the act: they echo each other's comments and play upon each other's words and in so doing create a special role for themselves, to the extent that their future appearances are characterized by conversation that is a cross between an antiphonal chant and an old-style vaudeville act.

A third shift of policy is one we will examine more fully in Chapters 2 and 3, an early predilection toward identifiable geography and chronology, which was to yield later to frames of reference that tend to be self-contained, without relationships with the real world and real time.

There are some others, which represent shifts away from the customary naturalistic crime story toward a narration that is not fantasy, not parody, not social criticism, but something else.

It is the "something else" that qualifies the 87th Precinct series for study in some depth. Consequently, this book will not undertake to deal with the total output of Evan Hunter or even of Ed McBain (though somebody should, and undoubtedly will), but only with this series as an instance of especially skillful handling of material by a popular novelist.

Anybody who has read many police stories is sure to detect a difference in the very "feel" of the 87th Precinct series. That difference is largely a matter of *tone*, that is, of the author's attitude toward his reader. Ed McBain, in these novels, is no realist, not at least in the sense that John Creasey, Maurice Procter, and Hillary Waugh are. What McBain does with a great deal of his material is to turn it just a little off-axis instead of giving it to us head-on. The result is a kind of obliquity that does not distort the picture, or throw it out of focus, but rather moves the camera-angle to a point from which everything is still clearly visible but just a little asymmetrical.

The most obvious instance is the orientation of the Imaginary City, created by taking a familiar geography and rolling it over by a quarter-turn, so that everything is still where we expect it to be, except that we are now seeing it on the slant. The canted impression is intensified by the new set of names assigned to the geographical features, which sound more like Podunk than a big metropolis: Bethtown, Calm's Point, Black Rock Span. Not as obvious, but following the same principle, is the tilt McBain gives to his time-frame, whereby the basic calendar seems accurate right down to the day of the week, but people age at different rates, and sometimes even segments of the past are thrown into a slanted perspective.

A little earlier we mentioned the introduction of Monoghan and Monroe in place of the standard tough city detective, as evidence of the "something else" of the series. Monoghan and Monroe are not just a pair of flaky characters; they are conveyors of an atmosphere that expresses itself in their speech-rhythms and word-play and continues to assert itself when they are not around: the pawn-shop owners in *Lady Killer,* the painters in *Fuzz,* and the garbage men in *Blood Relatives* keep the game going with a momentum obviously not inspired by any effort to portray such people as they would appear in real life.

There are other evidences we will discuss later, like the playfully double-barrel titles of many of the books and the eccentric minor characters who show up at the most unpredictable moments .

The limits of the slanted angle are stated clearly enough in that disclaimer at the beginning of each book:

> The city in these pages is imaginary.
> The people, the places are all fictitious.

But note carefully what comes next:

> Only the police routine is based on established investigatory technique.

There is no obliquity in the handling of police methods, which is one of the recognized strengths of the series, nor is there any distortion in the representation of the police sub-culture. The same can be said of the main characters in the story, who are certainly not caricatures, but we begin to feel the tilt as we move away from the center of the action, in the makeup of such people as Monoghan and Monroe, the Deaf Man, and Richard Genero.

Further along we will have several occasions to mention the special sense of reality in the 87th Precinct stories, which is based upon the off-axis angle just discussed and has the special virtue of allowing narrative necessity to take precedence over conventional "realism" for artistic purposes, as it does, for example, in the switches of themes in certain stories, in the types of crimes the police must deal with, and in the ethnic and sexual makeup of the detective squad itself. It also facilitates the ironic tone of much of the series, which has occasioned so much praise from critics who have recognized it and so much damnation from those who have not.

One quality of the 87th Precinct series that requires no expertise to recognize is the way McBain has refused to let himself be caught in a strict formula as a result of his own successes or the dictates of the conventions of the genre. This quality is particularly remarkable in so prolific a writer, who would find it much easier to produce book after book, each cast in the mold the public seems to like. Instead of undertaking to duplicate his successes, McBain mixes his plays like a skillful quarterback, almost invariably surprising us by catching us off balance. We will see how he varies his approaches in such things as the precision of the dating of the stories, in the types of plots and motives, and in the ways in which the people in the stories change. One thing we will not find is any stereotyping of people or situations.

Ed McBain would be a much easier writer to discuss if his work could be conveniently grouped into periods of development, as does the output of many writers. To read *Ice* immediately after *Cop Hater* is to be aware of a tremendous maturing of perceptions and skill, but I doubt if it would be possible to divide the intervening works into "periods" or "phases," each showing a common set of influences and directions. What we have, instead, is a gradual growth almost free of perceptible transition.

The plan of this book is as follows. Chapters 2 and 3 will be discussions of McBain's special handling of the geography and the chronology of the 87th Precinct stories. In Chapters 4-6 we will deal with the qualities of the novels as mystery fiction, particularly as police procedural stories, and with the nature of the police, the public, and crime. Chapters 7-10 will be devoted to the big four, those members of the Eight-Seven Squad who play the leading roles. The other regulars and those who make occasional appearances will be discussed in Chapters 11-13. Chapter 14 is devoted to the literary qualities of the saga, and the final chapter to some observations on the limitations of the series.

This book is intended for people with a variety of aims and tastes, ranging from the person with a general interest in mystery fiction all the way to the confirmed McBain addict. Recognizing that there is a certain amount of material which may appeal to the loyal McBainian but not necessarily to others, I have consigned to appendices such matters as the internal arrangement of the precinct station house and a detailed listing of police casualties.

Documentation will be held to a reasonable minimum. I have never subscribed to the notion that a footnote is an affront to human sensibility, but the fact is that the material dealt with in this study is so voluminous that most of the sentences that follow could each be referenced to two or more sources. Consequently, besides the customary attribution of secondary sources, footnoting will be used only in those instances that seem to call for additional explanation or amplification, and for those references that may be subject to question or controversy.

Readers who like to be taken completely by surprise at the conclusion of a mystery should be cautioned that it will be necessary to reveal the outcomes of some of the stories. I really doubt, however, that this practice will be so crucial with the McBain reader as it would be in the case of a straight puzzle-story fan.

Chapter 2

The Imaginary City

The statement appears at the beginning of every edition of each novel in the 87th Precinct series:

> The city in these pages is imaginary.
> The people, the places are all fictitious.

The reader who misses these sentences (as most undoubtedly do) should have no problems with setting; the story reads like a New York police story, and although he may experience some slight disorientation when McBain's cops investigate a murder on Culver Avenue or drive over to Calm's Point for an interview, our reader will have the same New York feel as in the Norah Mulcahaney stories of Lillian O'Donnell.

There are several recognizable reasons for the New York identification. By combining references from various stories, we can locate the Imaginary City with considerable precision. We know from *Killer's Payoff* that it is south of the Adirondacks; from *Lady Killer* that it is north of Norfolk, and from *The Heckler* that it is south of New Bedford; in 1965 it was about two hours' flying time from Chicago (*Doll*). There are a number of other such indicators, and they all place the Imaginary City in the immediate neighborhood of New York. The geographical size is about the same, and so is the population; some people in the City even talk like New Yorkers, referring, for example, to a public restroom as "the terlet."

The outline of the Imaginary City is more readily sensed than visualized. Anybody who undertakes to draw a map based purely on the descriptions in the stories may soon find himself baffled by the picture of a large metropolis located on the Atlantic coast, where the ocean is in the wrong direction and the two rivers that are such prominent geographical features flow the wrong way.

For reference purposes, three maps are included in the present text. The first is a sketch of the layout of the 87th Precinct, locating those streets, avenues, and other features that appear in the stories. The second shows the borough of Isola, in which the 87th is found, in relation to the two major rivers and the neighboring sections of the Imaginary City itself. The third map reduces the scale sufficiently to include those outlying locations that have figured in the series.

The reader familiar with the outline of the New York City area will perceive immediately how these maps were drawn. One needs only to rotate the real city ninety degrees clockwise, so that north becomes east, east becomes south, and so on, in order to produce a useable outline map of McBain's Imaginary City. All that is necessary is to substitute names: the Hudson (which, please note, now flows in a westerly direction) becomes the Harb, the East River becomes the River Dix, and the Harlem River becomes the Diamondback River. Manhattan is now called Isola, the Bronx is Riverhead, Queens is Majesta, Brooklyn is Calm's Point, and Staten Island (more properly, Richmond) is Bethtown. Other identifications should fall into place with relative ease. Sand's Spit, the long peninsula extending away to the east, is obviously the transmutation of Long Island, and the state to the north across the River Harb, always called "the next state" in the stories, is just as obviously New Jersey.

The City is a huge metropolis that had a population of eight million in 1957 and ten million in 1962. Some idea of geographical size may be gained from the fact that the driving time from Dover Plains Avenue in Riverhead to downtown Isola, in daytime traffic and observing all speed limits, is forty-two minutes. Travel by subway is understandably slower: in the late 1930s Detective Bert Kling, then of high school age, needed an hour and a half to travel from his home in Riverhead to an address in Calm's Point; in 1976, by the way, the same trip required about the same time. The City has at least two major airports; at the time of *The Mugger* it had six daily newspapers, a number that had been reduced to four in *Fuzz*.

Because Isola is the most populous of the five boroughs

and because the 87th Precinct is located close to the center of it, we will examine this crowded downtown area first and in some detail. Isola is a long, narrow island with its major axis oriented east-west, bordered by the River Harb on the north and the River Dix on the south. These rivers, by the way, are the only geographical features pictorally represented in the stories. In *The Mugger* there is an outline map of the little riverside park where Jeanne Paige's body was found, showing, among other things, the direction of the flow of the River Harb, and in *Jigsaw* is the photograph taken from the Isola end of the Calm's Point Bridge, in which a considerable expanse of the waters of the River Dix is clearly (or rather, dirtily) visible.

One difference between Isola and Manhattan is that the avenues in Isola run east-west, the numbered streets north-south. The imaginary island, though, has inherited certain features of the real one, and this trait may bother the reader until he understands how it works. When the people of the Imaginary City speak of going "downtown," they mean *west*, not *south*. Thus, one travels "up" to Riverhead (east), or comes "down" from Riverhead (going west). North-south travel on the island is "crosstown." Things get really confusing in the case of a reference to some place **"upstate"**, presumably upstate New York, but directionally off somewhere in the vicinity of Massachusetts. Another legacy of the Manhattan original is the habit of people in the stories of referring to "the city" when they mean only Isola; thus Roger Broome, when he remembers that the City is surrounded by water, is obviously thinking of Isola alone. It is part of the sportive tone of the series that McBain not only recognizes but frequently comments on these disparities, suggesting that the City is after all no more illogical than Tokyo or Biloxi.

The 87th Precinct (Map 1) is located close to the center of Isola, in a narrow strip between the River Harb and Grover Park. The precinct territory is only a few blocks wide[1] but thirty-five blocks long east to west. We are told at one point that the rule of thumb is one linear mile per twenty city blocks, giving us a precinct about a quarter of a mile wide and a mile and three-quarters long. The awkward shape produces such monstrosities as the patrolman's beat of thirty blocks of river-front in *The Heckler,* but even more seriously it places the police station house on the extreme southern edge of the precinct, just across the street from Grover Park, which is in the territory handled by the 88th and 89th Precincts.

The eastern and western boundaries of the precinct are never precisely defined, although we do know that the Alexander Hamilton Bridge, which crosses the River Harb to the north into the next state, lies near the eastern limit of the Eight-Seven, and since access to the bridge is on North Fifty-Sixth, this street must be the boundary. In the other direction, Silvermine Oval, which is inside the 87th Precinct, is a mile and a half from Hamilton Bridge and must be barely within the western boundary. Incidentally, since the precinct station house is close to Seventh Street, it seems probable that police headquarters is located not only on the southern extremity of the precinct territory but in the southwest corner of the area. The southern boundary, which coincides with Grover Avenue, along the northern edge of Grover Park, is the most definite of the precinct's territorial limits, although even this one does tend to shift a bit in a couple of the stories.[2] The northern boundary of the Eight-Seven territory is the riverfront of the River Harb, though in one story it moves south a block to Silvermine Road.

The 87th Precinct is a critically overcrowded urban area, with a population in 1956 of ninety thousand and the highest crime rate and the busiest fire department in the world.[3] Law enforcement is in the hands of a police force of 186 patrolmen and sixteen detectives.[4]

Specific locations within the Eight-Seven are usually identified by reference to the main avenues (which, remember, run east-west in the City), whose names soon become as familiar to the reader as if they were in his own city. In several of the stories, McBain takes us on a quick tour from the banks of the River Harb to the edge of Grover Park, reinforcing our orientation to the avenues within the precinct territory, as shown on Map 1. Immediately south of the river we cross the River Highway, which runs the length of the island along the edge of the River Harb.[5] A short stretch of this thoroughfare shows on that map in *The Mugger*, at the point where it intersects the access to Hamilton Bridge. The River Highway is one of the main traffic arteries from the high-cost residential areas into the downtown section, and that is why it was the

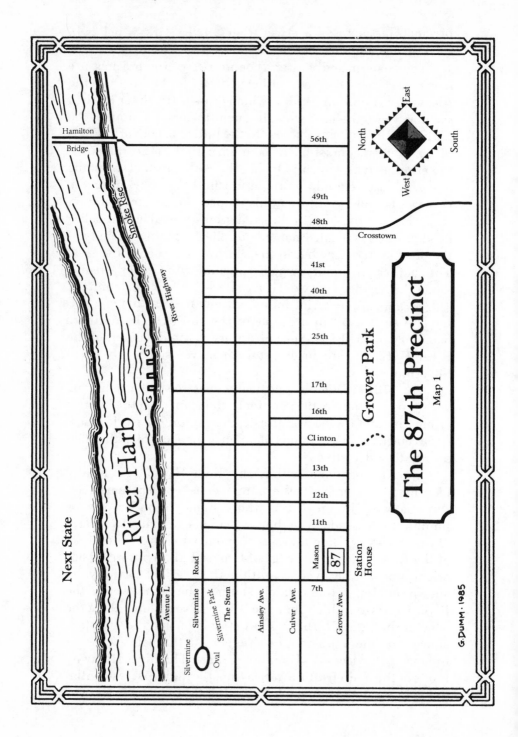

scene of the car-bomb explosion that killed Deputy Mayor Scanlon in *Fuzz*. Continuing this trip southward, the reader will next cross Silvermine Park and then Silvermine Road, lined with fancy apartment buildings that have the advantage of facing both the park and the river. The next street, however, is the Stem, gaudily commercial with its delicatessens and movie houses, representing a sharp drop from the affluence of Silvermine Road. Immediately south of the Stem is Ainsley Avenue, lined with old buildings that are still trying to maintain their former dignity; Ainsley, it will be remembered, was the location of Silvio Corradini's grocery, where the proprietor was killed and Detective Andy Parker wounded during an armed robbery. The incidence of violent crime on Ainsley, however, is minimal in comparison to that of the next street, Culver Avenue, which has been by far the scene of more of the crimes reported in the series than any other location in the 87th Precinct: as early as *Cop Hater*, it was in a bar on Culver that Bert Kling was shot with a zip-gun; as recently as *Ice*, it was on Culver that the Dirty Panties Bandit held up a laundromat. Between these two stories, at least a dozen murders and an assortment of cases of theft and assault have been reported on Culver Avenue.

Unlike the avenues we have just named, all of which run the length of the precinct and beyond, Mason Avenue is only three blocks long, but its reputation is just as strong as theirs, though considerably less savory. Mason is a slum in the Puerto Rican section, better known to the local inhabitants as "La Via de Putas" and to the police as "Whore Street" and "Hooker Heaven," which titles identify the nature of its sole industry. Just to the south of Mason is Grover Avenue, which marks the northern edge of Grover Park and the southern boundary of the precinct.

The reader never gets a corresponding tour through the precinct from east to west, partly because such a trip would take too long (thirty-five blocks) and partly because we would be crossing only a succession of nondescript side-streets, most of them numbered and virtually undistinguished from each other. A possible exception would be Clinton Street, on which, at its northern extremity, Roger Grimm's warehouse stood until it was burned in *Bread*; its southern end faces the Clinton

Street footpath into Grover Park, where the police tried to trap the Deaf Man with an empty lunch pail in *Fuzz*. Otherwise, we should make only two additional observations regarding these streets. The first is that the numbered streets end just a few blocks west of the precinct house which, it will be remembered, is close to the corner of Grover and Seventh; when Meyer and Willis set out from the precinct station, working their way west in a search for the man who was planning to kill "the Lady," they soon found themselves below First and among the named streets in the direction of downtown Isola. The other particular is that Culver Avenue is the dividing line between north and south addresses: thus, the drug store where Roger Broome bought a valentine for his mother is at the corner of Ainsley and North Eleventh, and the Hotel Carter is at Culver and South Eleventh.

A city, though, is more than a gridwork of streets and avenues; it is also a patchwork of affluence and poverty. Even within the relatively narrow limits of the 87th Precinct we find extremes of destitution and prosperity, often within the same neighborhood. The most affluent area within the Eight-Seven stretches along the shore of the River Harb, from Silvermine Oval eastward along Silvermine Road, where the tall apartment buildings still have elevator operators and doormen, all the way to that little pocket of extreme wealth lying within the fold of the river, Smoke Rise. Just to the south of the opulent belt, however, the areas blighted by poverty begin to make their appearance. There are slums right on the fringes of Silvermine Road, and along Ainsley Avenue the gradual change from riches to rags becomes quite perceptible. Culver Avenue is a stretch of almost completely unrelieved poverty along its entire length within the precinct. There are middle-class neighborhoods, but they do not get much attention in the stories; people who want a nice middle-income residential territory, like most of the detectives in the stories, live up in Riverhead or over in Calm's Point. There is, however, enough economic variety within the precinct to provide settings that range from the desperate poverty of *Long Time No See* to the lower middle-class of *See Them Die* to the middle-middle of *Blood Relatives* to the upper-middle of *Sadie When She Died* and to the extreme wealth of *King's Ransom*.

We should not leave the 87th Precinct without a special word about Smoke Rise, which is not only a geographic feature of the area but an economic phenomenon. Not far to the west of Hamilton Bridge the River Harb bends southward before resuming its westerly course, creating a small pocket between the river's shore and the River Highway. This area, exclusive, wooded and moneyed, is divided into some three dozen estates, and is called The Club by everybody except its own residents.

There are two other pockets of wealth within the Eight-Seven. The old Scott mansion, where Steve Carella investigated a murder in *Killer's Wedge,* is on the shoreline of the River Harb, but some distance west of Smoke Rise. At the western edge of the precinct territory is Silvermine Oval, not nearly so affluent as Smoke Rise, but at least a distantly wealthy relative. As we will see presently, Silvermine Oval is testimony to the adage that wealth does not necessarily breed serenity; people in that well-heeled neighborhood kill each other with distressing frequency.

Outside the Eight-Seven but still within the borough of Isola, the geographical feature of greatest significance is Grover Park, which hems in the precinct on the south.[6] This is a park of some considerable size, possibly as large as Central Park in Manhattan. It is big enough to contain a zoo, a lake, and a carousel, not to mention statues of Daniel Webster and General Pershing.[7] Grover Park is a crime-ridden area, and it is one of the frustrations of the detectives of the 87th Squad that the park territory, which is just across the street from the precinct station house, is not within the Eight-Seven's jurisdiction, a state of affairs that almost resulted in the death of Steve Carella on one occasion when a patrolman from another precinct failed to recognize him and blew his cover during a drug bust within the park.[8]

The southern edge of Grover Park is defined by Hall Avenue (Map 2), usually described by City folk as "swank" and "plush" and considered a much safer area than Culver or Ainsley. Hall Avenue, like Fifth Avenue in New York, is the traditional scene of the annual St. Patrick's Day parade, and one speaks of a "Hall Avenue debutante" in much the same frame of reference as the New York counterpart. Just one block south of Hall is Jefferson Avenue, which has become

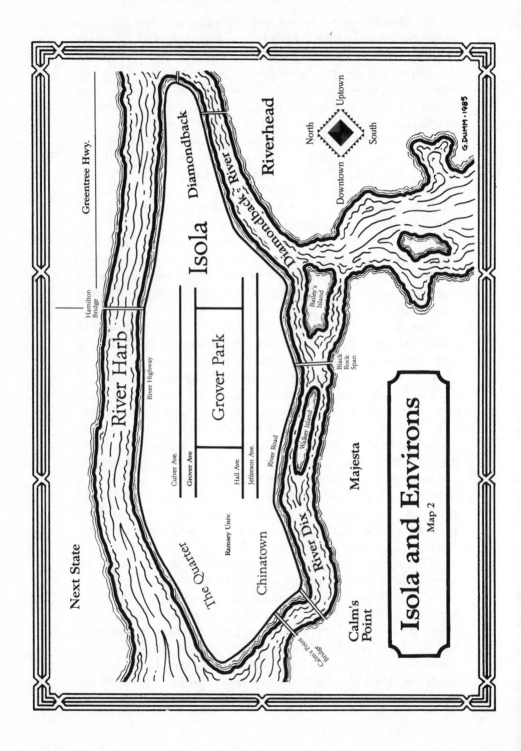

emblematic of the advertising business to the extent that "Jefferson Avenue advertising executive" is a familiar byword.

Another area that is geographically outside the 87th Precinct but still featured in the stories is Diamondback, the City's largest black ghetto, on the extreme eastern edge of the island of Isola. Diamondback was the scene of the race riots of 1935, and it is still described as "an area as deadly as a coiled rattlesnake." Although Diamondback is predominantly black, it contains other ethnic pockets, like El Infierno, a realistically named Puerto Rican neighborhood. The action in the stories does not spill over into Diamondback as frequently as into an area like Riverhead, a circumstance for which the cops of the 87th Squad are usually thankful, because Diamondback is the location of the 83rd Precinct and Detective Ollie Weeks, whom they prefer to avoid.

Away in the other direction, close to the westernmost tip of Isola, is the Quarter, usually described as the bohemian or avant-garde community, in the extreme downtown section of the City. The Quarter is an area of little theatres and starving actors, of artsy-craftsy shops and off-beat arts. The action of the stories frequently shifts into the Quarter, especially in *Give the Boys a Great Big Hand,* where the mystery surrounds the disappearance of the stripper, Bubbles Caesar, who worked at the King and Queen night club.

The southern border of the Quarter touches the edge of Ramsey University, of which we will have more to say a little further along, and immediately south of Ramsey is Chinatown, an area of the old city that encompasses more than one ethnic neighborhood, particularly the Straits of Naoli, or Little Italy. Probably the best remembered location in Chinatown is Charlie Chen's tattoo parlor, where Teddy Carella got her first tiny black butterfly in *The Con Man* and went back for the second one in *Ice.*

The one very affluent neighborhood in Isola outside the 87th Precinct is Stewart City, which is three square blocks of super-swank apartment buildings located on the south side of the island, on the River Dix. We get some idea of the oppressive exclusiveness of Stewart City when Detective Bert Kling goes down there to interview Ted Boone and is scorned by the elevator operator.

The section of the City that is the scene of more action in the stories than any other outside the 87th Precinct itself is Riverhead, the largely residential borough across the Diamondback River to the east of Isola. One reason why so much of the narrative development takes place in Riverhead is that Steve Carella and his family live there, which circumstance determined the scene of the murder and several attempted murders attendant upon the marriage of his sister in *'Til Death*, and in other stories the several attacks upon Carella himself in the vicinity of his home. Then, too, Riverhead is closer to the 87th Precinct than any other borough, with the result that the action frequently spills over there, as it does in *Ten Plus One* and *Hail to the Chief*. As a matter of fact, Dover Plains Avenue in Riverhead has been the scene of as much of the action as any street in the 87th Precinct, except Culver Avenue.

West Riverhead, just across the Diamondback River from Isola, has fallen victim to serious urban blight, with an unemployment rate of twenty-eight per cent even in good times, and with forty-two per cent of the population on the City's welfare rolls. Farther east, though, are good middle-income residential neighborhoods, with one-family houses and middle-class apartment buildings. Besides the Carellas, a number of other people in the stories have lived in Riverhead, including Claire Townsend and, at one time, Bert Kling.

Majesta, although it lies just across the River Dix from Isola, is almost inevitably considered an outlying section, remote and almost rural. The ticket-seller at the Majesta Ferry waiting room in Isola assures the Deaf Man that there will be no problem in getting his truck on the ferry at any time, because not many people ever want to go over to Majesta. This, of course, was the reason why the Deaf Man located the operations base of his first big caper in Majesta, where nobody would take note of him and his confederates. It may also explain the location in Majesta of the neighborhood the police call Baby Bogota, which has become the base of operations of South American gangsters engaged in the cocaine trade. Although it has been long since connected to Isola by bridge, it is still considered to be far from the center of city life, and, as the narrator tells us, Majesta is not an elegant section: "In fact, it is what you might call crappy."

Calm's Point, the other largely residential borough, has suffered the same bucolic reputation as Majesta. In spite of the fact that it has always been joined to downtown Isola via the Calm's Point Bridge, snobbish Isolites habitually refer to it as the "Calm's Point sticks" and "the City's hinterlands." It has its slum areas, like the notorious Clearview, but it also has exclusive Calm's Point Heights (familiarly, "Cee Pee Aitch"), with gaslit lamp posts and cobblestone streets, and it obviously has some good solid residential areas, because Lieutenant Peter Byrnes of the 87th Squad lives there.

Bethtown, located on an island west of Isola across the bay that comprises the City's harbor (Map 3), is the local equivalent of Siberia where the police are concerned. When a dumb patrolman interferes with Meyer Meyer's pursuit of the sniper in *Ten Plus One,* Meyer's ultimate threat is to consign him to the fate of walking a beat in Bethtown, and Lieutenant Byrnes promises the same destiny to Genero if he does not get rid of his noisy radio. The Bethtown Ferry, "the poor man's ocean crusier," was once the favorite ride of dating couples who could not afford the City's more expensive entertainments. Now, however, Bethtown has become the last of the boroughs to be joined to the rest of the City by a bridge.

Outside the five boroughs of the City proper, the land feature mentioned most often is Sand's Spit, a peninsula that extends almost due eastward from Calm's Point and Majesta, which are really located on its western end. We know that Sand's Spit is a body of some considerable size, because the beach at Westphalia, where Bert and Gussie Kling attended that fateful weekend party in *Heat,* is a hundred and thirty miles from the City. Once a land of potato farmers and a few exclusive resort areas like Sand Harbor, Sand's Spit is being suburbanized by the expanding city, to the extent that it is called a "middle-class slum area" at one point. Typical of the change is Morristown, which grew up as a housing development in the post-World War II years, and nearby Shorecrest Hills. Sand's Spit does, however, serve two important functions besides supplying room for the City's overflow population. It has some of the most beautiful beaches

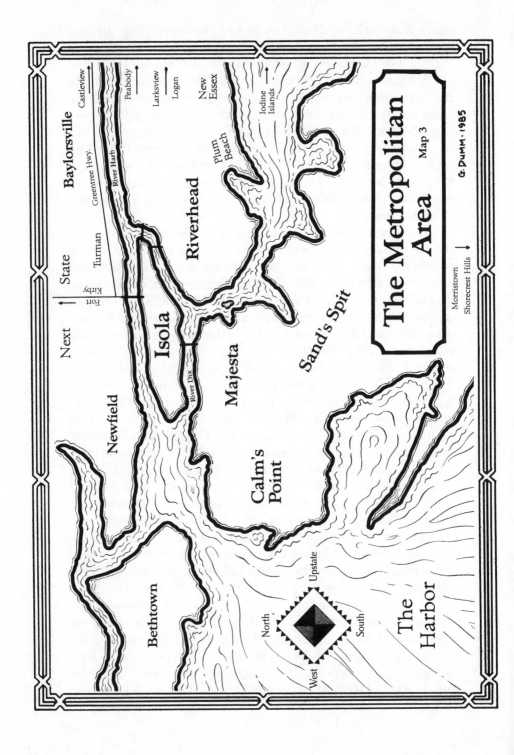

The Metropolitan Area   Map 3

G. Dumm · 1985

in the world, and it is a buffer against the Atlantic storms that would otherwise do some severe damage to the City and its suburbs.

In *Calypso* we learn of the existence of the Iodine Islands, clustered around Sand's Spit near the mouth of the bay that separates the peninsula from the mainland. The islands are six in number, one set aside as a state park, three developed with high-rise condominiums and hotels, the other two privately owned. One of these two is Kent Island, the scene of what must have been one of the most hideous murders in the history of crime.

Besides those suburban areas already mentioned, there are a number of other small towns close enough to downtown to be the homes of people who are involved in cases handled by the 87th Squad. Larksview, an exclusive suburb located about a half hour outside the City, was the home of the comedian Stan Gifford, who died suddenly during one of his television shows in *Eighty Million Eyes*. Larksview becomes a symbol of luxurious living to Blanche Lettiger, who is daydreaming about how it would be to live there just before she is killed by the sniper in *Ten Plus One*. Peabody, home of Lucy Mencken in *Killer's Payoff*, must be on about the same economic level as Larksview, and so must Logan, about forty minutes from downtown, where arsonists burned Roger Grimm's home in *Bread*. Somewhat further down the social scale is New Essex, about fifteen miles east of Riverhead, the home of George Lasser, who was superintendent of an apartment building in the 87th precinct (*Ax*).

Several other suburban towns are located across the River Harb to the north, in that area always referred to enigmatically as "the next state." The designation is really a feasible one, because to call it frankly New Jersey would create such contradictions and dilemmas as to shake the reader loose from the illusion of the Imaginary City. At any rate, when a person crosses the Hamilton Bridge into the next state, he may bear left into the town of Newfield, or right onto the Greentree Highway, which will take him up the River Harb past Castleview-on-Rawley, where the state penitentiary is located. If our traveler proceeds straight ahead (north) after emerging from Hamilton Bridge,he will presently find himself in

Turman, will then pass through Baylorsville, and, if he continues on this route for forty miles, will reach Fort Kirby, where Major John Francis Tataglia was stationed.[9]

Before leaving this discussion of the layout of McBain's City and its environs, we should make some mention of the relationship between crime and geography in the stories. When we come to Chapter 6, we will observe that the incidence of those crimes on which the stories are based has a considerably smaller relationship to such matters as social status and race than to the necessity for telling an interesting and original story. The same principle applies to the geographical location of the assorted crimes, which are far less dependent on economic status and ethnicity than other factors. A few paragraphs earlier we mentioned the fact that Culver Avenue and its immediate neighborhoods have the highest crime rate in the City in terms of numbers of crimes that actually supply the plots for the stories, but we should add at once that many of those crimes are not related to the poverty areas on and around Culver, or the ethnic backgrounds of their residents. Part of the large homicide rate on Culver has been created by the fact that it is the location of the Browser Bookstore, where a gunman killed Claire Townsend and three other people at one time, part by the circumstance that two of the victims of the sniper in *Ten Plus One* were gunned down on Culver, and part by its having been the scene of the double homicide in *Jigsaw,* none of which was directly related to the blighted Culver Avenue neighborhood. Another good case in point is "La Via de Putas," Mason Avenue, with its wide-open prostitution and its general atmosphere of degradation. In the stories, wealthy Silvermine Oval has been the scene of considerably more crime than Mason Avenue, not because wealth breeds more crime than fornication does in real life, but because murders in well-appointed residences (like those of Sarah Fletcher and Jeremiah Newman) are better story material than those committed in Hooker Heaven.

To the question, Isn't the Imaginary City actually New York? there must be two answers, Yes and No.

Obviously, it is New York. What else can we call a place located on the East Coast, three and a quarter air hours north of Miami (in 1957), four hours fifty-five minutes east of San

Francisco (in 1968), and called "the biggest city in the richest country in the world"?

At the same time, McBain on several occasions takes considerable pains to separate the two. In *Lady Killer* (18) Fats Donner tells Cotton Hawes a certain pusher he is seeking has gone to New York, and twice later in the same story the *New York Times* is pointedly called an out-of-town paper (39-40, 55). The same kind of conscious effort appears in *Ghosts,* when a woman tells Carella her husband is in *"the* city, man," an obvious reference to New York (162).

The people in the stories almost inadvertently put the City back where it belongs, however, in their frequent offhand references to Macy's and Gimbel's and in lapses like the one of Cotton Hawes when Carella asks him to put in a call to Sarasota: Hawes replies, "Sarasota? Where's that, upstate?" and the reader need not consult an atlas to catch on that Hawes is thinking of Saratoga. We can, of course, add such details as Edward Schlesser's remark, "My business is here, but I live in Connecticut," or Luis Ordiz's arrest record, showing that he was arrested and tried in the Imaginary City and sentenced to four years "at the state penetentiary, Ossining, New York," or Mrs. Hernandez's statement that when Anibal flew up from Puerto Rico, "We pick him up at Idlewild." If the City and New York are not the same, they are so incredibly close together as to be essentially one.

One practical certainty is that New York, like an inadequately exorcised ghost, will continue to haunt the Imaginary City as long as the stories appear. Consider, for example, the curious behavior of "La Via de Putas," Mason Avenue, which runs north and south in *Cop Hater,* so that a suspect lives in a "house at the corner of Culver and Mason," then settles into its proper 87th Precinct orientation parallel to Culver through a considerable number of stories, but swings back to its north-south position in *Ice.* This kind of thing is an almost inevitable result of a maneuver like that of rolling New York over on its side and changing all the familiar directions, especially with such a complicated geography to handle and so many details to keep straight. Most readers will not even notice the fact that Sand's Spit runs "pristinely north and south" in *Calypso,* leaving its east-west direction to seek its old identity as Long Island.

When we turn to the social-cultural character of the City, one factor that impresses us at once is the considerable number of colleges and universities within its borders. There is Women's University, where Claire Townsend studied social work, Haworth University, where Dr. Carl Nelson graduated, and Amberson Women's College, where Meyer Meyer gave his memorable lecture on rape prevention. The school that most often enters the picture, however, is Ramsey University, which is located in the downtown area right next to the Quarter. Besides being the scene of that production of Eugene O'Neill's *The Long Voyage Home* back in 1940 which triggered such disastrous consequences twenty-two years later, Ramsey was also the alma mater of Klaus Scheiner (*So Long As You Both Shall Live*), Jonathan Newman (*Heat*) and Timothy Moore (*Ice*).

Because of the hazardous nature of police work, hospitals naturally become the scene of more action than do the centers of learning. The one that is featured most often is Buena Vista (sometimes written Buenavista), where both Steve Carella and Richard Genero were confined in *Fuzz*, and where Andy Parker was taken after he was shot during the grocery story holdup in *Hail, Hail, the Gang's All Here!* Claire Townsend worked at Buena Vista for a while, and so did Cindy Forrest, who broke with Bert Kling when she fell in love with a psychiatrist on the staff there. One reason why this hospital is the scene of so much action is that it is convenient to the 87th Precinct, but another is that it is strong on treatment of narcotics cases, and it has a good psychiatric ward. Another convenient hospital is Isola General, where Carella almost died in *The Pusher*. Still another, which hovers on the edge of the action in the River Dix is the Dix Sanitarium for drug addicts, located on Bailey's Island, near the prison. Names of a great many others appear in individual stories, like Bramlook psychiatric hospital, Elizabeth Rushmore, Sacred Heart in Calm's Point, old Hanover, and Worth Memorial, down in Chinatown.

Prisons unfortunately figure heavily in the stories, the one most familiar to the reader being Castleview, which becomes the residence of most of the criminals who are successfully apprehended by the boys of the Eight-Seven. Castleview is located at Castleview-on-Rawley upstate, in a beautiful setting on the bank of the River Harb. Within the City, incarceration is accomplished at Bailey's Island, which we just mentioned in connection with the hospital, or at nearby Walker Island, also in the River Dix.

A study of the linguistic habits of a population is often a clue to the more general aspects of a culture, and we fortunately have enough samples of the speech patterns of the inhabitants of the City to make a few observations. We have already noted the tendency of certain residents to use the pronunciation "terlet," to which we might add the "deses and doses" that are reported to be characteristic of the accent of Calm's Point.[10] The City, being a melting-pot of many ethnic elements, has naturally developed dialectal patterns, to the extent that the speech-sounds of certain areas are almost unintelligible to outsiders. Most of these local accents are described as harsh and unpleasant, especially those of Isola and Calm's Point, and the speech of Riverhead, in its unrelieved form, is considered to be a decided social handicap.

The history of the City comes through in little snatches here and there, usually in the form of a brief anecdote explaining the origin of a place name, or an explanation of some historical landmark. Most of it sounds as if it came out of Washington Irving's *Knickerbocker History*. In *Lady, Lady, I Did It!* for example, we are given an account of how the five boroughs got their names. Isola was discovered by an unimaginative Italian explorer, who could not come up with any name more creative than "The Island." Bethtown, on the other hand, was settled by the English, and was supposed to have been "Besstown" in honor of Elizabeth I, but the emissary who delivered the name had an unfortunate lisp, and "Bethtown" stuck. Majesta was also an English settlement and was to be named in honor of George III, but the region was already over-supplied with Georgetowns, hence the name, derived from the Latin *majestas* (majesty). Riverhead was originally a Dutch settlement called Ryerhert after the patroon who owned the land, but the name was anglicized to "Riverhead" in 1917. A considerable mystery surrounds Calm's Point, which sounds as if it should have been named after somebody, but which, we are told, was not named after anybody.

The early history of the City seems to parallel that of New York: relics of the Dutch settlers still exist in street names like Goedkoop Avenue in the old section of downtown Isola, and in family names like Van Houten in Smoke Rise. Of the English takeover we can only guess, but the naming of Bethtown for the first Queen Elizabeth and Stewart City for the Stuarts would seem to indicate a date early in the seventeenth century. What part the City played in the American Revolution is an historical blank except for the presence of Nathan Hale Square in the center of Isola, and so is the first half of the nineteenth century, except for the founding of Ramsey University in 1842. As for the City's contribution to the Union cause in the War Between the States, it appears to have consisted in the participation of General Richard Joseph Condon, whose statue presently provides a roosting-place for pigeons in Condon Square, and who was noted chiefly for his unsurpassed wit, style, and grace. The Spanish-American War produced General Ronald King, who stormed a strategic hill in Cuba and whose statue now stands in Grover Park as a testimonial to the esteem of a mayor who shared General King's addiction to poker.

It was not until the First World War, however, that the City was caught up by anything approaching real patriotic fervor. That zeal apparently expressed itself in such an intense admiration for General John J. Pershing that his statue now stands in Grover Park, and in his honor the City changed the name of an avenue that had previously honored General Grant. It also manifested itself in the change of the good Dutch name of Ryerhert to Riverhead, on the ground that Ryerhert sounded too German.

Of General Herbert Alexander, whose equestrian statue graces Herbert Alexander Oval in Riverhead, we know nothing, except that he was most probably the ancestor of the editor of that name who once saved Steve Carella's life.[11]

The *feel* of McBain's City, in the context of both time and place, is the sense of New York City, to the extent that the reader who follows a story along St. Sebastian Avenue in Diamondback can feel himself on St. Nicholas Avenue in Harlem without loss of identification or orientation. At the same time, the reader will not forget very long that he is in a legendary environment where the ordinary rules of reality may not apply, where details that would constitute problems in a realistic story are simply bypassed without notice in the Imaginary City.

Not many readers would even catch the anomaly in *King's Ransom* where King and Carella, being directed by automobile telephone through the 87th Precinct toward the point where they are to drop the ransom money, are asked for their location. They report that they are approaching North Thirty-Ninth and Culver; the kidnapper's direction then is to turn left on North Fortieth, which they do. Having come from the direction of Smoke Rise, they are going *west*, and hence should pass Fortieth before they reach Thirty-Ninth, but the reality has been so thoroughly enveloped in the legend that no one notices the difference.

We can almost see the dividing line between legend and reality on those few occasions when McBain makes a deliberate cross-over between the two worlds. *Killer's Payoff* was an early effort to relate the story to the external world, even to the extent of inclusion of a map of the Schenectady area, showing real towns that figure in the story. Cotton Hawes in that book drives across the Hamilton Bridge into the "next state," where he heads north along the shore of the River Harb, on his way to *upstate New York*. Now, this is what anybody would do driving from the real Manhattan to Schenectady, but it is most decidedly what could not be done in the Imaginary City, because such a route would lead away from the river and into the hinterlands. What Hawes does, actually, is to cross the shadow-line that separates fiction from fact, whereupon he is headed in the right direction. Of course this cross-over happens in almost every story when people travel between the City and Philadelphia or Boston, but the shock of transition is muted by the fact that it takes place off-stage.

After the early novels in the series there is a perceptible lessening of transits into the real world, evidently indicating a change of strategy on McBain's part. References like the one to the state penitentiary at Ossining and to Schenectady disappear from the later stories, with the result that the search for an old murder in *Ghosts* takes Steve Carella and Denise Scott to the fictitious "Hampstead," Massachusetts, instead of a real place. What has happened, apparently, is that a series that began with a conveniently invented setting, much like the "Granchester" of Maurice Procter's stories, has established its own identity and no further explanation of the relationship to reality is necessary.

The illusion of reality is created in large degree by the mass of circumstantial detail. Everything is named, whether one of those throw-away addresses like "North Founders, just off Byram Lane" that appear only once, or Dover Plains Avenue in Riverhead, that has been the scene of so much of the action that we feel quite at home there. The total effect is a sense of place without physical reference: when we find ourselves on "Ashmead Avenue, in the shadow of the elevated structure in downtown Calm's Point, not far from the business section and the Academy of Music," we may not be able to locate ourselves on a map, but our senses tell us how it looks and sounds and feels on Ashmead Avenue in Calm's Point.

One really important thing remains to be said about the City: it is not just a setting, an arena devised for the acting-out of the stories. It (or more properly, *she*) is a leading character in the series. The City is repeatedly personified, always as a woman, and it is her moods and vagaries that very perceptibly influence the attitudes of the other characters and set the tone of the story. She is the object of a love-hate relationship that is specifically attributed to Steve Carella but bespeaks the attitude of the narrator and ultimately most of the other people in the story.

She appears on the first page of *Cop Hater,* not yet as a person but as locale:

> The city lay like a sparkling nest of rare gems, shimmering in layer upon layer of pulsating intensity.
> The buildings were a stage set.

The passage goes on to tell us that the shining gaudy buildings are a front, hiding the garbage in the streets behind them.

Notice, though, what has happened on the first page of *The Mugger,* which opens

> The city could be nothing but a woman....

And in *Killer's Wedge:*

> There she was—the city. All decked out for the pleasure of the night, wearing her sleek black satin with a bright red sash.

And *Fuzz:*

> The bitch city is something different on Saturday night....

And *Let's Hear It for the Deaf Man:*

> Take a look at this city.
> How can you possibly hate her?

Her presence is always felt, whether in those lyric passages like the ones just cited or in her more direct participation in the stories, seductively soft and sweet in spring and autumn, harshly cruel in summer and winter.

In an interview several years ago, Evan Hunter (speaking as Ed McBain) said, "The city in the 87th Precinct series is a distortion of the city in which I was born and raised: New York."[12] *Distortion* is not exactly the word. What McBain has done, actually, is to work a transformation that has preserved the best of two unities. The familiar setting is there, with changed directions and different names, but everything is just where we expect it to be, and it looks and sounds and smells exactly as it should. Superimposed on this reality, though, is another one that fits the picture and seems completely in focus, though at the same time capable of tolerating the various absurdities that we could never accept in New York City, or in any other real place, for that matter. It is a setting from which, without the overlay, we would have to exclude the Deaf Man, and Monoghan and Monroe, because they are too fantastic for the New York scene. With the double exposure, however, the stories will accommodate not only characters that seem at times slightly flaky, but even an imaginary calendar that lets time advance and stand still simultaneously.

Chapter 3

The Imaginary Year, the Elastic Calendar, And the Stopped Clock

Besides the 87th Precinct series, there are almost no other collections of mysteries for which a study of chronology would be appropriate or fruitful. One exception would be the Holmes stories, over which the Sherlockians seem to have endless fun arguing about their dating, but most writers either assign unequivocal dates to their accounts or ignore the business of chronology entirely.

We are devoting a chapter to the chronology of the 87th Precinct stories for two reasons. First, the subtle handling of the time-element, which is so unobtrusive that it is for the most part quite imperceptible, is unique in suspense writing. Also, the chronological element follows much the same plan as that of the geography we have just discussed, to the extent that they both become parts of a rather remarkable overall pattern of actuality. That pattern reinforces the sense of "tilt" we mentioned in Chapter 1, the special slant on reality that needs to be recognized in order to gain full appreciation of McBain's narrative technique.

Just as every street in the Eight-Seven saga is named, so are most events dated. The practice begins in *Cop Hater,* when the first murder takes place on Sunday, July 23, and it is continued with the exact dating of *The Mugger,* where it is "Tuesday, September 12" and so on through the story, and into *The Pusher* with "Monday, December 18" and other specific dates. The only information not supplied is the year, and if we become curious about what year it is and consult the real calender, we make a remarkable discovery; it isn't any year, despite the fact that those dates sound so precise and reliable.

Here is how it works out. If we start with the 1956 calendar (which would be logical, since the books were published during that year), we discover that we are a day off: July 23 (a Sunday in *Cop Hater*, remember) fell on a *Monday* in 1956, and so with the corresponding dates in *The Mugger* and *The Pusher,* which are consistent with those in *Cop Hater,* and all a day too early for 1956. So (still being utterly logical) we try the 1955 calendar, only to find the dates a day too late: July 23 was a *Saturday* in that year. What happened, of course, was that 1956 was a leap year, which caused the days of the week to move up two days instead of the usual one, leaving a gap into which our author has inserted a whole fictitious calendar, and we may well believe that he has invented an Imaginary Year falling midway between 1955 and 1956, in the same way that he invented an Imaginary City located exactly where New York should be.

I believe the first critic to explore the timing and dating of the 87th Precinct series was William Bradley Stickland, who in an ingenious paper entitled "Of Time and the River Harb: The Chronology of the 87th Precinct" in 1979[1] worked out a detailed time-scheme for the series, to which I am indebted for many of the facts and ideas in this chapter. My own dates differ from Professor Strickland's in several instances, but if the reader would care to work out a system for himself, he will undoubtedly find that it differs from both Strickland's and mine.

In Appendix E "An Eighty-Seventh Precinct Chronology," I have made a quick summary of all the stories in the saga, from *Cop Hater* to *Ice,* placing them in order of occurrence (which is not always the same as the order of publication) and setting dates for the beginning and ending of the main action of each. As we have just noted in regard to the first three books, McBain's "years" do not always correspond to real-calendar years, and in those cases I have translated the dates to fit the non-fiction calendar.

By the way, the very business of fixing the time-limits is an illuminating exercise with respect to McBain's ability to create an illusion of the passage of time. *King's Ransom* is a good example: it is surprising to find that the story actually covers only an eighteen-hour period, because it seems so much longer. There are flashbacks to the events of recent days, plus an epilogue more than a month later, but the time-frame of the plot is from early evening of one day to noon of the next. The impression is even stronger in *Long Time No See,* where the action is completed in six days, but where the brooding sense of the past suggests a story bridging several years.

The Imaginary Year, which must be translated as 1956, the year of the publication of the first three stories, runs through *Cop Hater, The Mugger* and *The Pusher,* with major events precisely dated by day of the month and the week. The practice is interrupted in *The Con Man,* in which we are told only the month: we know it is the April after *Cop Hater,* but nothing more definite. Then comes another series of three (*Killer's Choice, Killer's Payoff,* and *Lady Killer*) dated by day of the week and day of the month, all dates corresponding to the real calendar for 1957.

Killer's Payoff, as a matter of fact, is one of two stories dated by year. At the beginning of Chapter 4 there is a facsimile of a savings account statement stamped "April 1957," and a few pages later a check dated June 23, 1957. *Killer's Payoff,* you will remember, is the only story in which there is any delineation of non-fictional geography (that map of the Schenectady area), and it is apparent that this story represents an early experiment with a kind of realism McBain later abandoned in favor of his own blend of fantasy and plausibility.

Significantly, these first seven stories give us more precise information about the ages of the main characters than we will see again. We learn that Steve Carella is thirty-four and Bert Kling twenty-four, and that Danny Gimp, the informant, is fifty-four. This is just about the last we will hear of these ages, though there is one about which we will hear a great deal for years to come: Meyer Meyer is thirty-seven.

Following the series of three definitely "dated" stories we next encounter three that appear to have been left just as deliberately uncertain. *Killer's Wedge* takes place on a Friday early in October. We can determine from internal evidence that the year is 1957: Cotton Hawes, for example, who transferred into the 87th from the 30th Precinct in *Killer's Choice,* has been on the squad four months.[2] The next story, *'Til Death,* contains an ambiguity that seems quite deliberate, especially so since it affects one of the most important dates in the series, the Sunday on which Steve Carella's sister was married and the day the Carella twins were born. What was the date of that Sunday in June? Was it the twenty-second, as the narrator tells us early in the account, making the year 1958, or the twenty-first, as it appears on the duty roster at the precinct station, making it 1959? In a later story June 22 is confirmed as the right date, but in the mean time we have had an intentional suspension of the practice of precise dating. The interruption is continued in *King's Ransom*, this time not ambiguously but with deliberate vagueness: the time is October, without any hint of day of the month or week.

In *Give the Boys a Great Big Hand* and *The Heckler* events are again dated by day of the week and day of the month, placing those stories in March and April, 1959. The events of *See Them Die,* however, take place on a Sunday in July, without reference to the calendar. Somebody in the story remarks on one event in *Give the Boys a Great Big Hand* in such a way that we know this one is the same year, but the interesting reference is Carella's comment that the twins were "a year old in June." The age of those twins will bear watching, because it is about to do some surprising things.

The novelette *The Empty Hours* must be placed next in point of time. Although it was published a year later than *Lady, Lady, I Did It!*, it obviously pre-dates the murder of Claire Townsend.[3] *The Empty Hours* is the second story with the year (1960) designated, and it will be the last. In this one, Meyer Meyer is thirty-seven, as he was four years ago when he came upon the scene in *The Mugger.*

The Empty Hours is specifically dated August 1960, and the tragic events of *Lady, Lady, I Did It!* followed, in October.[4] This is another of the benchmark stories in the series, because Bert Kling and the other men of the squad will remember for many years the massacre in the Browser Bookstore, where Claire Townsend and three other people were gunned down. One fact hammered home throughout this story is that the mass murder was perpetrated on Friday, the thirteenth; as a matter of fact, October 13 fell on a Thursday in 1960, but no matter. This is our first experience of the Elastic Calendar which, like the Imaginary Year of the beginning of the series, is flexible enough to let Friday fall on the thirteenth, whether it actually did or not, without in the least disturbing the credibility of the story.

Beginning with *Lady, Lady, I Did It!* we have a series of five stories (including the novelette *"J"*) with both days of the week and day of the month given, corresponding to the calendars for 1961-64. In these, Meyer Meyer is still thirty-seven, and if we wonder who is lying, it is not Meyer. The narrator confirms Meyer's age, registered now and for many years to come on a clock that has stopped.

This would seem to be a good place to comment on the novelette *Storm*, which was published within the same year as *The Empty Hours* and *"J"* in 1962, and which is detached from the 87th Precinct saga in both time and place. This is the story in which Cotton Hawes takes Blanche Colby up to Rawson Mountain, in that anomalous "upstate" region, for a week-end of skiing and other diversions but spends most of his time helping the local police solve a couple of murders. Chronologically, *Storm* presents two problems. First, it is hard to reconcile the story with Hawes' highly developed ethical sense: he had fallen in love with Christine Maxwell during the investigation in *Lady Killer* and continued to date her for many years afterward, so that his perfidy in this case is decidedly un-Hawes-like. In terms of chronological placement the story is impossible. We know that it is winter, but there is no reference to month or day, and the only allusion to contemporary events is a statement that Hawes had transferred into the 87th Precinct some time earlier. Actually, the only thing we can say with any confidence is that Meyer Meyer was thirty-seven when these events took place.

The sequence of five "dated" stories, through *Ax*, is interrupted by *He Who Hesitates*, in which the entire action is seen through the eyes of an outsider, Roger Broome of Carey, a small town "upstate." We are told only that it is the day before Valentine's Day, but the year is obviously the same as that of *Ax*, which is 1964, and a little additional exercise in logic will confirm that the day is Thursday, February 13.[5]

Beginning with *Doll* and continuing through *Jigsaw* we have another sequence of five novels with day of the week and of the month, fitting the pattern of the real calendar. If we are fussy about such things we may be puzzled by the fact that the Carella twins are a year too young in *Doll* and two years too young in *Shotgun*, but as we will see shortly, those twins are aging on a track of the Elastic Calendar that does not necessarily match the standard time-frame.

Once again the sequence is interrupted by an "undated" story, this time by the pert *Hail, Hail, the Gang's All Here!* in which McBain runs his entire cast on stage and breaks the series record for the number of plots within one book. All these events are encompassed within a twenty-four-hour period, a Sunday in October, with no indication of the day of the month. Fortunately for the chronologer, there is the arrest record of a criminal who was last sentenced in November 1970, so that this one may be confidently dated in October 1971.[6] Meyer Meyer, it should be noted, is thirty-seven in *Hail, Hail, the Gang's All Here!*

Beginning with *Sadie When She Died* and continuing through the next eleven novels is a series precisely dated by day of week and month, each fitting the calendar for the year assigned in the "Chronology" of Appendix E, with the exception of *Let's Hear It for the Deaf Man*, where it must be April 1973, though the calendar dates are those for 1971.[7]

Now, however, some really amazing things begin to happen to the age of the Carella twins, who, as we have already noted, seem to have slipped back two years in *Shotgun*. When we find those two writing letters to Santa Claus at Christmas 1971, thirteen years after the date of their birth, we begin to suspect that their calendar has stopped turning, and we should thus not be surprised when, in February 1982, almost twenty-four years after their birth by real-world time, they are still only ten. What McBain has done, obviously, is to follow the pattern of certain comic strips (*Blondie,* for example) in which the children age at a consistent rate up to a convenient stopping-point and hold there.

There seems to be a design in the alternation of dated and non-dated stories, which changed as the series progressed. Note however the early pattern is a sequence of two or more stories conveniently dated (day of the week, day of the month), interspersed with some dated uncertainly (*The Con Man*), ambiguously (*'Til Death*), or circumstantially (*He Who*

Hesitates). Soon, however, the practice turns toward definite dating. Stretches of "dated" stories are broken first by three indefinite ones (*Killer's Wedge, 'Til Death, King's Ransom*), then one (*See Them Die*), one again (*He Who Hesitates*), and one more (*Hail, Hail, the Gang's All Here!*). Since these interruptions we have gone through eleven stories *all* with their dates easily identifiable with the non-fiction calendar. Note also, however, that only two early stories contain specific references to the year: *Killer's Payoff* (1957) and *The Empty Hours* (1960). Apparently this practice was abandoned because it tended to interfere with the illusory passage of time, just as those inadvertent references to New York interfere with the illusion of the Imaginary City.

If indeed we have not caught on earlier, we must become aware in *Bread* that time in the 87th Precinct is moving at various rates, when Steve Carella makes reference to his "nine-year-old son Mark," whereas more than a year earlier in *Let's Hear It for the Deaf Man* he had recalled the day his sister married "more than thirteen years ago," a remarkable state of affairs in view of the fact that Mark and April were born on the day of their father's sister's wedding. Carella's memory for dates is not especially good, but it becomes obvious that something more fundamental is at work here: the twins are not aging at the same rate as time is passing on other tracks.

Actually, there are four kinds of time in the stories, or, more accurately, time in different contexts moves with at least four different speeds.

First, there is calendar time, which the police use in their reports and in other situations calling for specific dating. It provides the context for those exchanges so frequently incidental to the action, "That was last Wednesday, right?" "That's right, April fifteenth." As we have seen, this time-track usually corresponds to the external calendar, though it is flexible enough to allow for the placement of a year between 1955 and 1956. It will even let December 22 fall on a Friday in one year (as it does in *Ghosts*) and July 31 on a Thursday in the following year (*Heat*), a mathematical impossibility on the non-fiction calendar.[8] In the stories, this kind of time is perfectly plausible because its mechanics are never obvious.

Then there is the time-track on which the main characters

(except Meyer) age. Time on this track does not move at the calendar rate, because such aging would make Carella (who was thirty-four in *Killer's Choice*) fifty-nine in *Ice*. Bert Kling, on the same scale, was twenty-four in *The Mugger* and would have been forty-three at the time of his marriage. Consider also what would have happened to Danny Gimp, who was already fifty-four back in 1956. The reasonable assumption is that (especially in view of the fact that none of their ages have been mentioned since *'Til Death*) they are growing older at approximately *half* the calendar rate, which would put Carella in his mid-forties now and would have made Bert Kling about thirty-three in *So Long As You Both Shall Live*. The ages of people like Teddy Carella and Peter Byrnes are never given, but it would seem reasonable that they are growing older at the same rate as the others.

The Carella twins represent an interesting variation: not only are they aging on a different time-track, but theirs slows down and finally stops as the story progresses. For five years (up to *Ax*, 1964) Mark and April age on schedule, according to the calendar. The next time we see them (in *Doll*) they have fallen a year behind, and in *Bread* the lag has increased to seven years. At that point, they stop growing older; they have been ten since *Blood Relatives*. To the reader, of course, the age of the twins is completely satisfactory, as is that of their father. What kind of impression would it make for an almost-sixty-year-old Steve Carella to come home from a hard day on the job, to be greeted by his twenty-four-year old children? As McBain says, I ask you now!

The fourth kind of time is the age of Meyer Meyer, who was thirty-seven back in 1956 and has been thirty-seven every time his age has been mentioned since. In *Hail, Hail, the Gang's All Here!* Mrs. Gorman estimates Meyer to be around forty-five (which would be about right if Meyer were aging at the same rate as the others) but he corrects her, and in *Calypso* he simply ducks a question about his age. We are told repeatedly that Meyer is prematurely bald as a result of his boyhood tensions and that his baldness makes him look older, but the explanation is really unnecessary: Meyer's clock has stopped.

It is apparent that there is both purpose and pattern in this manipulation of time-frames. McBain's intention is to create a chronology that has the dual advantage of seeming to be precise and regular while at the same time subject to control. The plan becomes evident upon examination of those many cross-references between the stories, particularly those in which characters try to remember how many years have passed since a certain event took place. Not surprisingly, the story most often recalled in later novels is *'Til Death*, because everybody remembers that Sunday in June when Carella's sister married, Cotton Hawes was beaten insensible by Oona Blake, and the Carella twins were born. The second most frequent benchmark is *Lady, Lady, I Did It!*, the story of the death of Claire Townsend. The many recollections of these two sets of events would seem to offer a reliable guide to a chronology for the 87th Precinct saga, but in reality they do nothing of the sort, because of the deliberate ambiguity built into the dates of both stories. *'Til Death*, it will be recalled, is dated both June 21 and June 22, and although the doubt is later removed, the suggestion of uncertainty is still there. The same is true, in a different context, of the date of the murder of Claire Townsend, which is insistently Friday, October 13 in a year when that date is impossible. When Steve Carella, working on the murder of another young woman, recalls the "bullet-torn body of Claire Townsend . . . not four years ago" the reader has a feeling of precise accuracy, though that certainty will vanish if he tries to pin down the exact year.[9]

The pattern of casual ambiguity becomes clearer when we bear in mind that there have been two stories (*Killer's Payoff* and *The Empty Hours*) explicitly dated by year; these two would make first-class reference points for subsequent stories except that nobody ever recalls the gangland-style killing of Seymour Kramer or the perplexing murder of Josie Thompson/Claudia Davis. The same is true of the two stories in which the year is clearly inferred: *"J"* (when Easter eve and April Fool came on the same day, 1961) and *Ax* (when 1904 was sixty years ago). There are no later references to the events in *"J,"* and only one to *Ax*, just a month later and hence no help in long-range dating.

Readers occasionally notice what must be a conscious avoidance of a too-tight consequentiality between the stories. More than one sharp-eyed observer, for example, has wondered what happpened to that elaborate plot cooked up by Bert Kling and Claire Townsend in *The Con Man* for Claire to take her exams early so she and Bert could have their vacations together (98-103); in *Killer's Choice* (51-2) Claire is taking her exams on schedule, and she and Bert make no mention of their cherished caper. One must also wonder at the way Steve and Teddy Carella ignore their own wedding anniversary. Investigating the murder in *The Empty Hours*, Steve takes Teddy along for a drive up to Triangle Lake on a beautiful Sunday in August, at just the time of year they had married, but they let the occasion go by without a single thought of its special significance. The fabric that unites the series is effective, but it is not obsessive.

McBain's time-framework is a gorgeously intricate topology which conveniently stretches in one dimension and contracts in another, always creating the impression of firm reliability and at the same time refusing to be pinned down to any tame conformity. As paradox, it harmonizes with the comic spirit of the series and is entirely appropriate to the mildly deranged world in which Monoghan and Monroe not only remain on the city's payroll but seem to prosper, and in which the sinister Deaf Man owes his life to poor dumb Genero.

The parallel is especially strong, though, between the chronology and the geography of the stories. In both dimensions, plausibility is achieved by means of specificity of reference: exact days of the week and month are set side by side with addresses complete with house number and name of street. The same kind of effect is achieved with regard to spans of time and stretches of space: an event is recalled as happening so many years ago (or even so many months or days), and one location is said to be so many miles, blocks or minutes of driving time distant—always with a confidence that keeps the reader firmly oriented with respect to both time and place. Naturally, the very sense of specificity glosses over the inconsistencies, so that Friday, October 13, 1960, is no problem, any worse than crossing 39th Street before we get to 40th while driving toward downtown.

The assertion that the mystery story creates its own reality has almost become a truism of mystery criticism, yet there is no way to describe more accurately what Ed McBain has been able to create with respect to the passage of time in the 87th Precinct stories. We have already seen how the geography of the Imaginary City is essentially that of a closed world which really exists in a dimension separate from that of New York City, a world in which everything seems quite natural so long as we are moving and experiencing within the system, but which goes badly out of kilter if we try, for example, to decide where "upstate" is in relation to the City. The same principle applies to the passage of time. The reader has a sense of assurance when it is "Thursday, February 4," regardless of whether that date does indeed correspond to the calendar for last year, or whether the Carella twins are still ten years old (although we can remember when they were born, almost a quarter of a century ago), or whether Meyer Meyer has been thirty-seven for so long.

Chapter 4

Procedures, Routines and Pure Dumb Luck

The 87th Precinct stories belong to a type of mystery usually called the police procedural, a tale in which the problems are attacked by police detectives rather than eccentric genuises, gifted amateurs or private investigators. The "procedural" part of the name arises from the use of police routines (like stakeouts, laboratory analysis and informants) instead of brilliant mental or spectacular combative feats to solve the crimes.

From the beginning of the series, Ed McBain's understanding of the intricacies and involvements of police work, together with his awareness of their limitations, has consistently attracted favorable notice of readers who delight in those absorbing descriptions like that autopsy report in *The Mugger*, which culminates in a surprising revelation about the victim. The pattern is set in *Cop Hater*, where we find accounts of the use of the lineup in criminal identification, the formula for. determining the character of a man's walk from his heelprint, and the use of such repositories of information as the Lousy File, an encyclopedia of known criminals. All of these make gorgeous suspenseful reading and supply an atmosphere of plausibility that is rare in the mystery, but the reader may find himself jarred, after finishing the story, to remember that, in spite of all those highly scientific techniques, apprehending the perpetrator in *Cop Hater* is the result of luck rather than of painstaking procedure.

At this point the critic must be careful not to generalize on the basis of a single sampling. There are writers of mystery series who adopt a formula in the first book and follow it unswervingly thereafter, but not Ed McBain. As we have seen

41

in connection with the chronology of the 87th Precinct saga, it is part of McBain's style to vary his pattern, and we will see this habit repeated in a number of other features of the series. *Cop Hater* sets the tone of the later stories, but it does not establish a tight mold. Thus, for a commmentator to observe, as Stephen Knight does, that in the 87th Precinct stories, "Police work, with its detail and method, does often enable the detectives to rule people out, or catch the minor professional offenders in the plot, but it cannot close in on the human betrayers who pose the central threats ..."[1] is to jump too quickly in the face of too much evidence to the contrary.

The procedures employed by police detectives in procedural stories may be grouped into two categories. The first is the investigative technique based on the formal, organized knowledge of the science of criminology, the kind taught at the Police Academy, the kind that relies heavily on the work of the police lab and the computer. This was the methodology first used in a procedural novel by Lawrence Treat, who in his Mitch Taylor series introduced a police scientist named Jub Freeman, an expert in such techniques as the spectroscopic analysis of paint scrapings. The other is the kind of know-how based on cop-canniness, the skill in empirical deduction sharpened by years on the job and by the cumulative transmitted lore of other policemen. This kind of detection was a special strength of the police in the stories of Hillary Waugh, another pioneer in the procedural genre. As we will see, the cops of the 87th Precinct depend on both kinds of knowledge in the pursuit of the criminals in the stories, though they do tend to rely more heavily on the police lab and the prodigious police files available to them than do most procedural detectives. One reason for this inclination, no doubt, is the availability of the police laboratory in downtown Isola, operated by Captain Sam Grossman and his staff, and reported to be the best in the world.

In the actual telling of the stories, McBain shows two special strengths that have become trade-marks of the series. One is the precisely detailed, step-by-step account of an analysis or an identification, like the description of the reconstruction of a burnt match book in *The Heckler*, which has the virtue of adding plausibility to the narrative and at the same time building the suspense by the careful stacking of detail on detail, with that loving care which has endeared to readers the stories of Michael Crichton. The other absorbing device is the one that first shows up in *Cop Hater* in the final report on a bullet from Ballistics, the facsimile of the actual form with information inexpertly typed in, and later an arrest record also literally reproduced as it looked when taken from the file. Anybody interested in bureaucratic forms, by the way, might make up a fairly complete file of them from the series, from all those B-sheets, DD Reports, PD Complaint Reports, and a couple of dozen others that illustrate the series.

A few examples may illustrate the richness of the stories in those police methods that are at least supposed to lead to apprehending of criminals. First, we may recall the assorted descriptions of those several methods of tailing designed to keep a suspect in view and at the same time ignorant of the fact that he is being followed. In *Fuzz* we learn the ABC method, wherein Detective A follows directly behind the subject, Detective B follows A and keeps him in view, while Detective C moves parallel to the subject, an arrangement designed to cover unexpected changes in route and at the same time not permit the prey to recognize any of his shadows. A variation of this pattern is the isosceles triangle tail described in *Hail, Hail, the Gang's All Here*, conducted by two detectives following at equal distances. The bookend tail (*Heat*) places one detective ahead of the subject and one behind him and is useful in conducting surveillance on a subway train.

Several writers of procedurals use the work of the police artist in their stories, but only McBain has reproduced the exact results in a series of visuals. In *Lady Killer* there are four drawings of the same head, changed and developed as the witnesses make corrections and suggestions, and then the big final surprise in the police drawing with one feature added by the pencil of Cotton Hawes. McBain used the device once more, in a single drawing by the police artist of Cindy Forrest's attacker in *Eighty Million Eyes*.

The use of informants in detection is one of the basic departures of the police procedural story from the conventions of the older types of mystery. Informants are, in general, the best source of information to the police in the procedurals, as they reportedly are in real-life police work.[2] The two old reliables in the Eight-Seven are Danny Gimp, customarily used by Steve Carella, who made his first appearance early in *Cop Hater*, and Fats Donner, who usually works for Hal Willis and is first seen in *The Mugger*. The police are warm in their praise of the services of these sources of information, and the personal relationship between Danny Gimp and Carella is one of the closest in the series, but the fact is that both of them serve chiefly in a supportive or advisory capacity, the single exception being the part played by Danny Gimp in *The Pusher*, where he helps Lieutenant Byrnes identify Gonzo and thus fingers the attempted murderer of Carella. Recently, the biggest success has been scored by the newcomer, Francisco Palacios ("the Cowboy"), who manages to hold a prostitute in his porn shop until Carella can get there and question her (*Calypso*).

It is in the use of police laboratory science, however, that McBain really excels, and on occasion the accounts of tests and analyses are laymen's guides to the use of chemical and microscopic techniques in crime detection. In *Ice* Sam Grossman describes for Carella the tests he had used in determining whether some residue found in a victim's handbag could be cocaine: color tests, with names of scales and chemicals employed as reagents, tests for precipitation and crystallization, after which Grossman, true to his scientific training, will venture only that the powder was *probably* cocaine. This kind of attention to detail and credibility requires some painstaking work on the part of the author, but the outcome for the reader is a strong sense of truth and also a participation in the exercise of suspense, which holds our attention by the authority of accurate information. The murderer who hangs his victim by a rope in order to give the impression of suicide should also take note of the capacity of the lab for testing a rope's fibers to determine whether they were flattened downward (indicating fake suicide) or upward (indicating the real thing), as the police lab is able to do in the murder of Anibal Hernandez in *The Pusher* and in that of Jefferson Scott in *Killer's Wedge*.

Some of the results of microscopic analysis are even more spectacular, the most memorable being the accomplishment in

Eighty Million Eyes, where Grossman is able to break down a little wad of "glopis" (as he calls it) from a suspect's shoe into ten components, giving Bert Kling what amounts to a catalogue of his recent movements. All Kling needs is to find where a man might have walked to pick up suet, sawdust, animal blood, animal hair, fish scales, putty, creosoted wood splinters, copper filings, peanuts and gasoline.

This seems to be a good place to make special mention of Sam Grossman, head of the police laboratory, who is not a member of the 87th Squad but has been an important continuing character since the beginning. Grossman appears first in *Cop Hater* as an obviously competent police scientist, who explains to Carella the scale for determining age from the diameter of a human hair, and the agglutination tests for blood groups. Captain Grossman (who we learn was promoted to this rank in *Calypso*) is a literary descendant of Lawrence Treat's Jub Freeman in his professional approach to the practice of police science, but he is considerably more knowledgeable than Freeman. Grossman knows electricity as well as chemistry, and it is he who is able to construct a wiring diagram of the car bomb in *Fuzz*; he knows enough botany to use the scientific name of the orchid in his conversation with Carella in *Calypso*. He is also a trained detective who on occasion can come up with a valuable proposal unrelated to his scientific expertise, as when he suggests a motive for the murder in *Ax* or the reason for the knife being found in the bedroom in *Doll*. Besides his competence, Sam Grossman has a strong sense of compassion, and he makes a sincere (though unsuccessful) effort to help Bert Kling out of his emotional depression in *Ice*. His sense of humor is as well tuned as Meyer's, so that he loves to string out the telling of a joke (or the perpetuation of a practical gag) in order to achieve maximum effect.

We can get some idea of the quality of the police lab, and of police technology in general in the Eight-Seven Squad, by comparing the state of the art in the McBain stories with some others that are strong in this field. We have mentioned the kinship of Sam Grossman to Treat's Jub Freeman, and it is not really remarkable that the science of the 87th Precinct series surpasses that of Treat, because the Treat stories antedate them by several years and hence represent an earlier stage of development. The same can be said of the Harry Martineau stories of Maurice Procter, which also rely fairly heavily upon laboratory analysis and other such technologies. In Chapter 11 of the last Martineau story (*Hideaway*, 1968), Procter's police know a suspect has been in a certain cottage where he has obligingly left fingerprints and cigarette stubs, has leaned against paintwork in a tweed jacket and has picked up local soil in his trouser cuffs and on his shoes, hardly a dazzling achievement in comparison with what Grossman's boys are able to do with that wad of "glopis." Actually, a fairer match can be made between the McBain stories and the more nearly contemporary ones of Bill Knox, whose Glasgow police have access to the Scottish Criminal Records Office which, besides maintaining a first-class laboratory, also supplies the police with files of criminal conviction records, offenses conviction records, a Modus Operandi File and an index of 60,000 photographs and 200,000 sets of fingerprints.[3] These resources are obviously competitive with the information available to police in the Imaginary City, which consists of local files maintained by every precinct squad and by those prodigious files available from the Bureau of Criminal Identification downtown, that receives and classifies some 206,000 sets of fingerprints annually and answers requests for a quarter million criminal records. There is, however, one point on which Knox's police have a clear advantage over the Boys from Grover Avenue: the Scottish cops have access to the consultative services of Andrew MacMaster, Regius Professor of Forensic Medicine, Glasgow University, whose knowledge and ability in his field are considerably ahead of those of the assorted ME's of the Imaginary City.

We need now to return to the question suggested by the reference to Knight's *Form and Ideology in Crime Fiction*. How much of the detection in the 87th Precinct series is based upon consistent application of police principles and how much upon sheer dumb luck?

As I have pointed out elsewhere, the convention of the Fickle Breaks is one of the definitive components of the police procedural formula.[4] The pervasive influence of pure chance represents a decisive break with the classic tale of detection, where nothing must ever be left to chance. McBain's cops are like most of the others in fiction, constantly deploring the fact that success and failure in police work are dependent upon the breaks of the game. Quite often, of course, they are right. If Cotton Hawes had not drawn upon his own empirical knowledge of the way Christine Maxwell wore her underclothes, for instance, the murders in *Like Love* might have been written off as a double suicide, and if Kathy Folsom had not grabbed the microphone out of her husband's hand at the critical moment in *King's Ransom*, the kidnapping might not have had so happy an ending. These chancy outcomes are frequently the ones that stick in our memory because they are so dramatic, and they seem so right because of the predictable fickleness of the breaks in police work, with the result that we may tend to forget those occasions when regular police routines actually lead to solutions.

To what degree, then, is the success of police work in the 87th Precinct stories the result of chance? The question needs a little exploration, partly because it has an important bearing on the nature of the police procedural formula, and more especially in the present context because of what the answer reveals about McBain's method as a mystery writer.

Let's examine the balance between method and luck in the first seven stories, that group which first appeared in paperback between 1956 and 1958. As Stephen Knight points out,[5] the solution of the series of police killings in *Cop Hater* is almost entirely dependent on chance: if the third victim had not managed to wound the murderer with a pistol, and if the doctor who treated the wounded perpetrator had not read about the case in the paper, the police would never have been able to work up a description and a drawing of the killer. Even so, he is not caught until he tries to ambush Steve Carella, and Carella chances upon him in Teddy's apartment and takes him. We should not leave *Cop Hater*, however, without noting that the other crime in the story—the zip-gun shooting of Bert Kling—is solved by straight police work: Kling's assailant is one of those picked up because he had been missing from the earlier roundup of the teen-age street gang. Significantly, this routine success is played down, the whole account encompassed in a short paragraph.

In the next two, police methodology is decidedly the determinant factor. The most successful piece of detection in

The Mugger is done by Kling, still a patrolman, who undertakes a covert and unauthorized search for the murderer of Jeanne Paige. Apprehending the mugger Clifford, accomplished by the regular detectives of the 87th Squad, is dependent on luck only to the extent of Clifford's dropping a match folder at the scene of one of the attacks, but the rest is routine police follow-up that leads to the trapping of the mugger in the bar where he had picked up the match folder. In *The Pusher* we read those fascinating discussions of the types of fingerprints, the analysis of semen stains and the classifications of bird feathers, but none of these leads to the arrest of the triple murderer or of the drug dealer who shot Carella; instead, the chain of follow-through is from Carella's whispering the name "Gonzo" before he loses consciousness, to Danny Gimp's identifying Gonzo as Dickie Collins and finally to Collins' fingering the murderer of the Hernandezes and Dolores Faured. The detection is straight police work, though the clever lab business of semen stains and feathers is atmospheric scenery.

The Con Man almost falls back into the pattern of *Cop Hater*. The preparatory police work has been done, in this instance by Carella's alerting Charlie Chen to be on the lookout for a visit to his tattoo parlor, but the lucky conclusion of the case is the result of Teddy Carella's presence at Charlie Chen's at just the right moment, following the murderer and his intended victim, and leading her husband to the arrest. Police success in the minor plot (apprehending the two small-time con men) is, again, straight police work with almost no reliance on chance.

In the fifth novel, *Killer's Choice*, McBain does something he has not tried before, the use of the same pattern of luck and method in both the major and minor cases. The crucial break in the murder of Annie Boone is the sighting of an automobile by a drunk who, surprisingly, turns out to be a reliable witness. Ditto for the death of Roger Haviland, when the presence of Crazy Connie at the scene supplies accurate information on the getaway car. The rest of the action in both cases is a matter of following up and tracking down until the killers are nailed. *Killer's Payoff*, on the other hand, is almost entirely a combination of exercises in some good old-fashioned detective story style detection by Cotton Hawes and some sound application of police routine. Finally, *Lady Killer* is brought to a successful conclusion by a combination of a tremendous expenditure of police energy and some brilliant mental work by Hawes. Again, as with the clever lab work in *The Pusher*, we have that excellent but futile series of police drawings of the killer, which ironically leads nowhere in apprehending the prospective murderer.

It is impossible, really, to make any statement about the persistence of chance as opposed to the effectiveness of police method that will adequately cover what McBain does in the first seven 87th Precinct stories. The cops in the stories are always complaining about the fickleness of fate in their work, and the narrator joins the chorus several times, as he does in a fairly long passage at the beginning of Chapter 17 of *Killer's Payoff*, "You can carry deduction only so far," but the fact is that luck alone plays a crucial part in the outcome of only three of the stories: Carella's lucky arrival at Teddy's apartment in time to shoot it out with the killer in *Cop Hater*, Teddy's fortunate presence in Charlie Chen's tattoo parlor when murderer and victim appear in *The Con Man*, and the presence of reliable witnesses on the two murder scenes in *Killer's Choice*. Even so, we must remind ourselves that the turn of fate in two of these cases is influenced by human intervention: Teddy manages to signal Steve that the killer is waiting for him in her apartment, and Charlie Chen is able to add his efforts to those of Teddy because he has been alerted to the nature of the murderous con man.

The one thing we can say about the handling of the luck-versus-method theme is that McBain mixes his plays and refuses to fall into the mold of a tight formula. This variation of approach is, as we will see in regard to several other aspects of his narrative technique, a basic component of the McBain style.

This same pattern—or absence of pattern—also holds through that sequence of seven novels, beginning with *Blood Relatives* (1975) and continuing through *Ice* (1983). The murder of Muriel Stark is cleared up as a result of the lucky discovery of her diary in a garbage dump, plus some skillful interrogation of the most likely suspect. In *So Long As You Both Shall Live,* however, the rescue of Augusta Kling is the outcome of some excellent cop sense, this time on the part of Detective Ollie Weeks of the 83rd Precinct. The killer of the three blind beggars in *Long Time No See* is identified by a letter found in the locked box of a victim in the course of the police investigation, but he is finally nailed as a result of the lucky chance that he had been bitten by the seeing-eye dog of one of his victims. The element of luck is (almost predictably) absent from *Calypso*, where the path of the series murderer is pointed by identification of a minute quantity of sand found at the scene of one of the murders, and by some systematic follow-up of the routines of a prostitute, who is another of the victims.

Ghosts is an interesting departure, in that supernatural evidence is introduced into the investigation, but as with the earlier picturesque developments, it leads nowhere: Carella's trip to the old house in Massachusetts will stick in our minds because of the colonial spectres he encounters, but the really effective result of that trip is his discovery of a single important fact about the leasing of the haunted house. Luck plays a part when the perpetrator is caught running away from a pawn shop, but the groundwork has been laid in the police stakeout.

Method and routine are once again the factors in the solution of the mystery surrounding the death of Jeremiah Newman in *Heat*, culminating in some very astute observations by Sam Grossman. The parallel major plot in this novel, involving the infidelity of Augusta Kling, is resolved by Bert Kling, using typical police investigative methods in the same unofficial efforts as he made in *The Mugger*. Lastly, the series of murders in *Ice* is cleared up by a combination of patient research (Brown's review of Edelman's business affairs, plus the identification of the first woman victim) and a communal flash of inspiration (recognition of the importance of a pocket radio). The results of police activity in *Ice* have two qualities that are really summaries of the balance between luck and method in the series. First, two of the most important discoveries in the story—the relationship of the Anderson woman to a drug dealer and the means by which the murderer sustained his alibi—are only the indirect results of hard work: in each case the police are so busy pursuing a line of inquiry that they almost accidentally blunder onto an important truth.

The other characteristic is manifested in the fact that two of the murders in the story are unsolved at the end (unsolved by the police, but not for the reader), and the appearances are that one of them will never be solved, a reminder that in police work, in contrast to the conventions of the traditional detective story, a number of cases go forever unsolved. Characteristically, in *Ice*, the two minor cases (those handled by Eileen Burke) are solved by straight police work.

Here, as in the first seven stories, the variety is satisfying and the approaches reasonably surprising. Luck plays a major part in fewer than half the cases; in the others, the police lab shares honors with systematic routine, common cop-sense and even a little brilliant insight.

In the stories between these first seven and the more recent ones we can, of course, recall a number of classic cases of the operation of pure luck in the solution (or non-solution) of cases. There is, for example, the frustration of the Deaf Man's elaborate caper in *The Heckler* by a simple-minded patrolman who lusts after an ice cream pop. There is the perfect crime in *He Who Hesitates*, where the police not only fail to suspect that Molly Nolan's body is in a refrigerator at the bottom of the river but actually have no knowledge of the existence of Molly Nolan—followed, with characteristically heavy-handed irony by that other stroke of pure chance in *Shotgun* wherein Roger Broome drinks too much and hands the police a complete solution on a platter. We could not leave this part of this discussion, of course, without mentioning the often bizarre operation of luck in *Fuzz*, when fickle fortune seems to alternate between frustrating all the efforts of the police and then doing the same for the lawbreakers.

On the other hand, we must not forget those instances in which the detection is as pristine as that found anywhere else in the mystery story. There is Steve Carella's single-handed solution of the locked-room puzzle in *Killer's Wedge*, resulting from the application of some exceptionally sound logic; Carella achieves much the same kind of feat in *The Empty Hours*, in first clearing up the identity of the victim and then trapping her killer. There is the solution of the complex puzzle of *Jigsaw*, resulting in the apprehension of a series murderer and the recovery of the loot from a bygone bank robbery. We could add

a number of others in which luck—favorable or unfavorable—
plays almost no part in the final outcome.

To this point, we have not really named the one most
important feature of McBain's use of police methodology. The
basic difference between the 87th Precinct series and most of
the others lies not in the knowledgeable detail regarding police
routines, or the skill with which they are described, but rather
with their impact on the consciousness of the men and women
in the stories.

It is a stylistic device of McBain to work up some
marvellous account of a highly sophisticated laboratory
analysis or a remarkably astute piece of deduction by
somebody on the detective force and then to turn the spotlight
not on the direct outcome of the detection but on the effect of the
operation on the police, the victims and the villains involved.
Thus Steve Carella, reading the diary of Muriel Stark in *Blood
Relatives*, is annoyed primarily not so much by the ugliness of
the situation created between Muriel and her cousins, as by the
prurient adolescent corn written into her erotic experiences.
Thus Mrs. Gorman, who has subdued her pride of family long
enough to call Meyer Meyer to her Smoke Rise mansion to
investigate the intrusion of poltergeists, realizing that Meyer
sees through her flimsy scheme, can plead only, "You see,
Detective Meyer, there *are* ghosts in this house" (*Hail, Hail, the
Gang's All Here*, 70). And thus with special potence Augusta
Kling, when the police burst into the the room just in time to
save her from her psychotic abductor in *So Long As You Both
Shall Live*, has only one thought as Ollie Weeks puts two quick
bullets into her would-be murderer: The fat man is the only one
of the men who does not love her. We could point to any number
of other instances to illustrate the fact that the concern of the
87th Precinct stories is not so much with the practice or results
of police methodology as with the impact of those practices on
men and women.

Chapter 5

The Police and the Public

In a number of ways, the super-detectives of the old mystery story tradition have it a lot easier than do the cops of the procedural stories. For one thing, they seem never to be short of money. Sherlock Holmes and Hercule Poirot, being consulting detectives, are presumably paid for their work, but the amounts and methods of payment are usually left tactfully unmentioned. Philo Vance, with his inheritance, is delicately aloof from such things. The really mercenary one among them is Nero Wolfe, who must practice his profession in order to support his expensive lifestyle, but his fees are so large (and enough of his clients so wealthy) that there seems always enough to preclude any real financial worry.

Holmes and his successors have rather consistently enjoyed another advantage, the privilege of selecting the cases they will work on. Great intellects like Philo Vance and Ellery Queen exercise the right to choose, from among the cases of their hard-working friend or parent, those that appeal to their finely tuned tastes. Then, having solved the mystery, purged the community of its guilt and restored it to a state of grace, they retire from the scene forever: Holmes returns to his chemistry and his music, Wolfe to his orchids, and as a rule they never again see the people with whom they have dealt in their cases.

Not so, obviously, with the policeman. As a rule he is a product of a low income or lower-middle income environment, and police work is his means of paying the bills for himself and his family. Not only does he not have the privilege of choosing the cases he will work on, but he almost invariably has a heavier case load than he can handle with any degree of efficiency. And finally, when he has successfully closed a case (which he does not always manage to do), he has no place to withdraw to; he must live always with the consequences of his work, because he and his family are part of the community he is paid to protect.

Before we undertake a discussion of the place of the police sub-culture in the total community, it might be profitable to take a look at the public the police must deal with in the 87th Precinct stories.

A broad overview of society or the sense of the total community is not one of the strengths of the 87th Precinct series stories as it is, for example, in the Lew Archer stories of Ross Macdonald or the Travis McGee stories of John D. MacDonald. Rather, McBain's stories are played out before a backdrop of a public that is as diverse and complex as it is enormous. The reader, for example, always has a sense of the ethnic groups that make up the City's population, majority and minority, but they are always part of the background rather than obtrusive social elements. Even in a story like *See Them Die*, with its intense awareness of the ethnic consciousness, when the conflict is between Puerto Rican and Puerto Rican, the focus is still upon the individual person and his or her concerns.

McBain's public, in other words, is a composite of persons, each with qualities that distinguish him or her from every other. As we have pointed out, Ed McBain works in terms of people to the extent that he will not introduce the least minor character into a story without stamping that person as somebody memorable.

The public with which the detectives of the 87th Squad must deal is composed of people like the young woman who witnessed the shooting of Anthony Forrest in *Ten Plus One*; when Carella asks for her address, the one thing she wants to make clear is that she does *not* live in a Puerto Rican neighborhood. Or the milkman who discovers the horribly mutilated corpses in *Shotgun* and whose hope is that he won't be docked for the time he spends helping the police. Or the restaurant owner in *Eighty Million Eyes*, who gives Bert Kling some important information only because a serious crime is involved, but "for minor things, who needs to be a good citizen?" Or, for that matter, the bartender in *So Long As You Both Shall Live*, who is questioned by the anxious Kling when he realizes that Augusta has disappeared on their wedding night: the bartender replies that they kidnapped *his* wife too: "I wish now they woulda kept her." Each has his own self-centered concern, but more than that. Those special qualities McBain gives them are inevitably unconventional and usually more than a little on the quirky side.

Certain patterns do recur, like those assorted exotics and eccentrics who tend to show up in the midst of the most somber occasions and to inject enough absurdity to take some of the edge off the tragedy. One of these is Fred Hassler, the photographer in whose apartment the two bodies have been found, and who is experiencing his first visit to a detective squad room. Hassler is overwhelmed by the color and the excitement of the setting, the color in this case produced by a victim bleeding from a knife wound, and the excitement by a gaggle of more noisy people than the cops can handle. Another of the memorable exotics is Phil, the doorman at the Fletcher apartment on Silvermine Oval, who can't shut up; any question directed to him brings forth such a torrent of verbiage that it is almost impossible to get him to come to the point. The series is full of such oddities, who are not certifiable screwballs but are certainly not your run-of-the-mill ordinary citizens either. Most especially many of them are people we will remember after we have forgotten who committed the murder in the story.

The City evidently has its share of outright nuts: "More of them outside than in," Sergeant Dave Murchison remarks to Meyer Meyer, just after Meyer has escorted from the station house a lady who has been annoyed during the past several nights by visits from a gorilla wearing a top hat and carrying an ivory-headed cane. This is in *Hail, Hail, the Gang's All Here!* but we must have met that lady in *Cop Hater* when she came to the squad room to report that the cop-killings were being perpetrated by the cockroach-men. She was Miss Bailey then, but she shows up yet again as Miss Aldershot in *Ghosts*, this time to report that the murder was committed by Superman, wearing blue underwear and a red cape.

Just for the record, though, it should be noted that the

nominal crazies make a much more creditable showing. Crazy Connie (*Killer's Choice*) looks as if she deserves the name, but she is as a matter of fact the reliable witness who knows every car on the road and whose accurate identification leads the police to the killer of Roger Haviland. Crazy Tom in *Blood Relatives* earned his name as a result of his residency in the city dump, but he recognizes the importance of Muriel Stark's diary when he finds it, and he places in the hands of the police the one clue that finally breaks the case for them.

Before moving on to the "normal" (if the term is ever applicable) members of the public in the 87th, we should mention a device McBain has used twice, to fix an individual whose oddity is only borderline, in that he is not aware of the drollery of his own name. The first of these is Earnest Hemingway, the young narcotics addict in *The Pusher*, who can't believe there is anybody else with his name. The other is Stan Quentin, the change booth attendant in *Ten Plus One*, who is indignant that anyone would name a prison for him.

About the great mass of people who make up the cast of characters of the series we can offer two general statements immediately. The first is that as individual persons they are as sharply delineated and as memorable as the assorted nuts and exotics we have already mentioned. The other is that, as a group, they are almost unanimously and automatically hostile to the police.

Some of the hostility is to be expected, because it is ingrained in the social class to which its practitioners belong. It is understandable in the Puerto Rican street kid, who knows he should never trust the police, or the tenement dweller of any age, who could not care less whether the police ever capture the guilty party. It may, however, be more difficult to understand in certain occupational groups, where it seems almost automatic. Hospital interns are inevitably hostile to the police, like Dr. McElroy at Buena Vista Hospital, who pointedly informs Carella and Meyer that he does not intend to answer any questions and must get back to his patients, or the nameless intern at Washington Hospital in Riverhead who does not want his patient to be questioned by the police because the boy might die and he would be held responsible.

Landladies seem to comprise another anti-police sub-culture. The one in the apartment house where Hawes has a shoot-out with a suspect complains that she is fed up to here with cops: "*You're* the ones caused the trouble." Her sister in the business, who shows the police up to the room where the Deaf Man had been staying, is elaborately sarcastic in her co-operation: "Sure why not? I got nothing else to do but show cops rooms." The same can be said of garage attendants, all of whom seem to have been inoculated at birth with cop-hater vaccine. The one who gives Carella and Hawes such a hard time in *Killer's Payoff* has at least suffered the provocation of receiving a ticket for driving thirty miles per hour in a twenty-mile zone, but the one at the municipal garage who summarily rejects the suggestion that any of his men could have wired a bomb in the deputy mayor's car needs no affront to activate his dislike of cops.

One of the most difficult groups the police must deal with is those people who boil over with civic indignation when asked to give a little help. A one-time victim of crime, for example, seems to feel that the cops are forever in his debt for failing to be on the scene at the critical moment: "Where were you when my apartment was robbed last July?" The reproof may take the form of a lecture, reminding the policeman (as if he had completely forgotten) that it is the duty of the police to protect the innocent. Accusing the police of wasting the taxpayers' money seems to come easy to any member of the public who does not approve of anything the cops happen to be doing at any given moment.

Then, there are those who claim sensitivity to the special smell of cops. These are usually people from the humbler walks of life, such as bartenders and elevator operators, and people whose sense of smell has been sharpened by their own earlier brushes with the law. They are a sub-group of a large category of people who automatically consider themselves superior to the police. Another manifestation is the haughty tone of Douglas King, who demands that the FBI be called in at once because the local Keystone Kops are not equipped to deal with the kidnapping. The position is not exclusive with the rich and well-educated, however. The blind man who narrowly escapes attack in *Long Time No See* calls the police, knowing that they will not do anything about it because the police in the City never do anything about anything.

Besides those who think the police never do anything, there are those who think they do too much. These are the people like the mother in *Ax*, who is outraged because Carella asks her seven-year-old son a few questions: "We don't live in Russia, you know." Sometimes they have cause for complaint, like Art Wetherley in *Eighty Million Eyes*, who was given a preemptory order by Andy Parker and now wants to know if we are living under a dictatorship. At times their fear is grounded, like that of Stanislaw Janik, who had enough of storm troopers in Poland and will not co-operate unless he is presented with a warrant (*Let's Hear It for the Deaf Man*).

One recurrent illustration of the fickleness of the public is the family row the police are repeatedly called upon to arbitrate, often involving physical hostility between husband and wife, and usually taking the form of a wife-beating, though the wife may on occasion retaliate with a frying pan to the head. In almost all of these situations the police are called in or otherwise find it necessary to intervene and are almost immediately rejected by both parties, who are indignant that anyone would think they are fighting, because "We love each other." The police have learned to expect such inconstancy, as does Arthur Brown who, when he has failed to locate a missing husband, goes to the home to report his lack of success to the wife, only to find that the return of the "missing" husband is being joyfully and carnally celebrated by the couple, who had neglected to tell the police.[1]

Superficially, the public in the 87th Precinct series is not radically different from those in stories located in New York, London or Stockholm. Among most of them we meet the same fear and hatred of the police, the same insecurity and distrust. The difference with McBain's public is that the people of the Imaginary City tend to be more capricious and less predictable, to the extent that they are often as surprising as the story endings themselves. Sometimes their behavior is more ironic than unpredictable, as in that mad scene in *Fuzz* where everything imaginable goes wrong with an elaborate stakeout and the suspect is escaping. Willis in desperation yells "Stop, police!" and the subject stops dead in his tracks. This suspect's story, as it develops during the next few pages, is entirely different from what the reader has been led to expect, though the outcome is less surprising than anticlimactic.

As far as the criminal part of the public is concerned, the attitude of the 87th Precinct cops ranges all the way from the professionalism of Steve Carella to the sadism of Andy Parker. As Carella drives along the River Harb and looks across at Castleview State Penitentiary, he thinks of the people he has placed within those walls as "business associates," which represents the kind of objective attitude he is usually able to maintain, in contrast to Parker's delight in physically beating young Puerto Ricans. One element almost completely missing from the police attitude is sympathy of the kind felt by John Creasey's George Gideon, who pities those poverty-stricken people who have been driven by circumstance into lives of crime.

The real determinant in the attitude of the 87th Precinct detectives is resentment, based specifically on the financial success of criminals in contrast to the near-penury of most policemen. The bitterness surfaces repeatedly, as it does while Carella and Hawes are inspecting a blackmailer's Cadillac in *Killer's Payoff*, knowing they will never own one themselves, and when Carella and Meyer learn that a moderately successful pusher makes almost as much in a week as they do in a month (*Ice*).

They are not as vocal in criticism of the leniency of the courts as are the police in some other stories, though Carella remarks in *Ghosts* that laws designed to protect the rights of citizens also protect those of criminals. Curiously, none of them ever comments on the Miranda and Escebedo decisions, which are intended to protect the rights of persons under arrest and which are so widely deplored by policemen as hindrances to effective law enforcement. There are several observations on Miranda-Escebedo in the stories (including one favorable to the principle), but they are all stated by the narrator, not by any of the characters.[2]

In a great many police stories, the cops make it clear that they feel closer—emotionally, socially, culturally—to the criminals they deal with than to the respectable law-abiding citizens. In the stories of Nicolas Freeling and Janwillem van de Wetering especially, the police not only feel at home with the crooks but actually share an affinity with them, which makes the police think and react in much the same way as do their targets. The 87th Precinct detectives have a great deal to say about the difficulty of telling which is which, the cop or the crook, and they even recognize a whole system of values they share with the criminal world, but they stop short of identification.

"Symbiosis" is the term McBain uses to describe the relationship. While Cotton Hawes is questioning a young woman junkie in *Fuzz*, there is complete communion between them; they share a body of knowledge and a system of insights, with the result that neither tries to deceive the other, and they know exactly what to expect of each other. After the interview, though, Hawes leaves her without any personal involvement or any sense of guilt toward her or her kind, and without her reminding him of anybody he knows.

The immediate bridge between the police and the criminal society is the informer, and like every other being who tries to live in two worlds his position is an extremely dangerous one. Criminals hate stool pigeons more than they hate cops, and the criminal world is likely to go to extremes to make an example of a stoolie who has been found out, by subjecting him to a particularly brutal death and by marking his body in such a way that the point is not lost on others who may be tempted.

Thus, the person willing to risk the consequences must have some very strong motivation to become an informer. The position of Fats Donner is typical: Fats has a record, he persists in infractions like keeping an under-age female in his apartment, and he is too lazy to be a really aggressive criminal. Hall Willis, who uses Fats most of the time, takes advantage of all these conditions, by not hauling him in on any number of charges and supplying him with a small intermittent income for information that does not require much energy. Like all others of his profession, Fats is trapped. Kling calls upon him for some information on the church-bombing in *Hail, Hail the Gang's All Here!*; Fats demurs, not wanting to get involved in a really dangerous situation, and Kling threatens to take him to the D.A. When Fats explains that he may wind up with a broken head, Kling reminds him he should have thought of that before he became an informer.

Most informers, though, work for only one detective, like Danny Gimp, who seldom helps anybody but Steve Carella. Danny (whose real name is Nelson) informs partly because he needs the money and partly out of a loyalty to Carella that is really unusual. He expects to be paid, but his honesty will not allow him to accept payment until he has something to deliver. On one occasion, being broke, he asks Carella for twice his customary fee, promising at the same time that the next one will be on the house. Danny will push his luck with the police, but not with the underworld. When he worries about a hood who suspects him, Carella offers to throw a scare into the man, but Danny declines out of prudence.

On one occasion (*Ice*, 181) Carella shakes hands with Danny Gimp, but we are pointedly told that the police do not often do that. Nobody really likes a "snitch" and the detectives usually consider them necessary nuisances, to be allowed to run on a short leash, but always in position to be brought to heel at a moment's notice.

As for the police themselves, they constitute a community within the community, a sub-culture within the broader society. The detectives not only work together, but they and their families frequently maintain social relations. Shortly after their marriage, Bert and Gussie Kling have dinner with the Carellas on one occasion and with the Meyers on another. Most of all, though, they feel a mutual dependence that makes them an enclave against the outside world. They may fight among themselves, but they draw together in a solid front against any kind of threat from the criminal world or the community at large. Nothing unites them like an attack on one of their own, even the killing of a lousy cop like Roger Haviland or the wounding of one like Andy Parker. Violence against policemen and their families becomes a personal matter. When Bert Kling's fiancee is killed in the Browser Bookstore, the police do not call it the Bookstore Case or the Claire Townsend Case; it is the Kling Case.

The public expectations of police work impose certain officially sanctioned roles upon the police. One of these, which is sure to be mentioned in any consideration of the status of policemen, is that of the low-paid civil servant. The habitual underpayment of policemen has several undesirable consequences, besides the obvious tendency to attract inferior people into the profession. As we mentioned a few paragraphs earlier, their own financial status in contrast to the affluence of many criminals generates a resentment that conditions most of their dealings with violators. Obviously, poor pay, coupled with the natural opportunities of police work, breeds graft, a subject we will discuss at greater length a little later. There is one other consequence that must have considerable effect, the pervasive stinginess of the police department in minor financial matters. The detective is free to use his own automobile or to buy gas for a police car during an investigation, but the chances are that he will never get back a cent he spends for gas. Carella is careful to ask for a receipt for every quarter he spends at a highway toll booth, knowing he will need proof that those amounts were spent on tolls and not on hamburgers for his own refreshment.

Another role is that of heavy responsibility, as demanding upon policemen as it is upon physicians and involving even further-reaching consequences. Obviously, the cops are almost incredibly overworked. There are no days when the police force can shut down for a holiday, Christmas and the Fourth of July being busier for them than other days. Likewise, there is no regular weekly day of rest, as there is with most vocations: note that *Hail, Hail, the Gang's All Here!*, which is based on the diversity of problems the cops must deal with, is set within the twenty-four hours of a Sunday. The 87th Squad is so badly understaffed, moreover, that any one of its members is working on a half dozen or so other cases in addition to the one that is the center of attention in the story. While Carella is investigating the jigsaw puzzle case, for example, he is also busy on a dry-cleaning store holdup, a series of muggings, a pusher working a junior high school and several burglaries in Smoke Rise, besides having to get ready to appear in court for a couple of cases coming to trial. As a guardian of the peace, the police detective is never off duty. On several occasions the 87th Precinct cops remark on the fact that they must always carry their guns. They are forever on call, and the call may come in the middle of the celebration of Passover, as it does for Meyer, or of a proposal of marriage, as it does for Kling. No job is ever finished; the moment one case is cleared up, the others are still there, and more new ones are developing.

The other manifest role, the one most visible to the public, is that of the authority figure. The popular conception of the city detective as the big strong man perpetually engaged in crouching behind squad car fenders and shooting at evil-doers is based on television instead of real life, but the very presence of a policeman in one's living room is terribly upsetting to many people. Even that mild expression "routine investigation" which the cops use to cover all kinds of situations has come to strike terror into the hearts of the most blameless of citizens. There is, however, one kind of authority automatically conferred on a policeman which is a highly potent weapon. This is the possibility of making bad matters worse when somebody tries to obstruct his investigative efforts. The situation arises repeatedly in the stories where a potential witness refuses to admit the police, or supply information, unless he is presented with a warrant. The reply always is that the cop *can* go all the way downtown and get a warrant, but the annoyance in so doing will make him many times meaner than he is now. Landlords and apartment supers are especially vulnerable to this kind of police clout, because an irritated cop can spot no end of violations of codes, to the extent of calling upon the sanitation people or the safety people or the you-name-it people to shut down the premises. Consequently, these folk usually co-operate, as do bartenders and other entrepreneurs who do not care to have the cops snooping about the place and scaring away customers.

These are the overtly sanctioned, institutionalized roles of the policeman. In addition, the nature of the job has imposed on the cop some unofficial patterns of conduct, none of which is approved by the society he serves, but each of which is a product of the individual's relation to the police establishment.

First, there is the graft, an inevitable outgrowth of the combination of low salary, constant contact with shady characters, and the considerable authority vested in any policeman. Many of the more knowledgeable residents of the City seem to expect that a payoff is part of the game of dealing with the law, like John Begley in *Lady Killer*, who blatantly asks Hawes if fifty dollars will be enough to forget the charge. The corruptions of the police in the McBain series range from such innocent rackets as never paying for a cup of coffee in a restaurant where he is known (or a meal if he has his family with him) to going to bed with women victims and suspects, and to such highly developed schemes as the ones Roger Haviland had going at the time of his death, and the payoff Ralph Corey was extracting from the crap game in *Ax*. The practices are so widespread that only the best cops—like Carella, Meyer, and Hawes—are able to stay clear of them.

Another covert role imposed on the policeman is a combination of ambivalence and pretense. The ambivalence is basically a matter of commitment to professional ideals the cops usually do not hold. The young patrolman, for example, may sympathize with the curiosity of the civilian who wants to loiter at a homicide scene and watch the excitement, but his job demands that he order everybody to keep moving and to act as if he believes it. A similar division of loyalties asserts itself when he is called upon to enforce laws he does not agree with, such as the pornography laws, when he knows that pornography has come to be a socially acceptable form of communication. Finally, when he recognizes that he is an organization man, whose natural inclinations must be buried under the priorities of the System, he may come to feel that the cop side of his appearance is nothing more than a front.

Most devastating, though, is the feeling of loss of identity as a result of having been absorbed into the police establishment. Steve Carella is as professional as they come, but even he is struck on occasion with the sense of having ceased to be an individual. He feels it when he is lying in the alleyway that cold night in *Fuzz*, trying to decoy the young hoods who have been incinerating drunks: as a cop, he does not enjoy the constant characterization of the police on TV and in the movies as dim-witted clods, but "You got an image, you got one." Carella feels it that day when the telephone supervisor tells him she can not give out information to "a person." And he replies without thinking, "I'm not a person, I'm a cop." Bert Kling feels it even more immediately when he calls upon Nora Simonov and wishes he could be in her living room as a person rather than a cop.

There are a great many aspects of his job that a policeman will talk about, especially to other policemen and to members of his own family, and some he tends to keep to himself. We may gain some insights into the nature of the police sub-culture by taking a look at each.

They talk freely and almost endlessly about their low pay and the consequent graft, even joke about it. Usually they seem to assume that they are in the wrong job, that nobody in his right mind would go into police work. This attitude has its defensive uses, too, in the sense that when things are going especially badly the oft-repeated question, "Who the hell asked you to become a cop?" serves as a buffer. They have another defense in that cliche they use so readily, "We don't make the laws, lady, we only enforce them," to relieve themselves of responsibility for the standards of society. They complain at length about the way they are over-worked, about the loss of identity and submersion in the System in police work, and about politics in the department. Among themselves, they talk without much restraint about their closeness to the criminal world in attitudes and values.

At the same time, there are some subjects which they seem not to want to talk about but which are very much on their minds. One of these is the fear of violent death. There are constant reminders of the dangers inherent in police work, such as the fact that policemen find it difficult to get life insurance and that most policemen have unlisted telephone numbers. The fear is often as not compounded by a sense of guilt: when Carella is shot by the Deaf Man, the other members of the squad are sorry, but they are secretly glad it is Carella and not themselves.

Unless he is a complete brute like Roger Haviland or Andy Parker, the police detective never becomes completely adjusted to the effects of physical violence, in spite of his having to deal with it daily. Professionally, policemen are supposed to be like surgeons performing an operation and to disassociate themselves and the victims from the crime, but it does not always work out that way, as Carella and Kling are reminded at the beginning of *Hail to the Chief,* when they find themselves unable to stare very long into the open ditch containing the bodies of the massacre victims, one of whom is an infant.

One fear always before them but almost never verbalized is

the dread of being made to look bad. The results are especially evident in a superior man like Cotton Hawes, who suffers the worst torments a cop can endure when his stupid misjudgment almost gets Carella killed in *Killer's Choice*, because he knows everybody on the squad has heard about his blunder, and again when his colleagues find him trussed up in the sniper's hideout in *'Til Death* after losing a struggle with a woman. Fear of looking bad also affects the squad as a whole, especially when some external outfit is called in to do a job the locals normally handle, as happens when the D.A.'s Squad assumes responsibility for protecting the Deputy Mayor in *Fuzz*. The Deaf Man, who is remarkably sensitive to the weaknesses of the police, recognizes this fear and plays upon it. His recent capers have been designed as much to make the police look like simpletons as to get away with fantastic robberies.

Writers of police procedurals tend to be heavily aware of the relationships between the police sub-culture and the general society, though they understandably differ from each other in their relative emphasis on social backgrounds and relationships. In the novels of Maj Sjöwall and Per Wahlöö, Swedish society plays a role almost as important as that of the police, while in those of Michael Gilbert the police world tends toward self-containment, in the sense that the narrative thrust is customarily with the police and their concerns. Moreover— and just as predictably—writers vary considerably in their relative emphasis upon the assorted factors that affect the associations between the police world and the broader society. We have already noted some of these variations in John Creasey's strong emphasis upon George Gideon's sympathy for the poor of London, and in Janwillem van de Wetering's and Nicolas Freeling's treatment of the theme of affinity between the policeman and the criminal.

We can get some idea of the nature of Ed McBain's narrative approach by comparing a few of those subjects that get heavy attention in the 87th Precinct stories with some others that are more strongly emphasized by other writers.

The first part of this consideration—McBain's points of emphasis—should be immediately apparent to any 87th Precinct addict who has read many of the other procedural writers. McBain is strong on relationships between the detective squad and the public, especially in his use of those transient meetings and associations between the police and the remarkable assortment of people who drift across their stage of action. He is also heavy on the inferior status of police work, the insufficient pay and the corruption and graft into which policemen are drawn as a result.

One topic McBain has avoided is the police union as a response to the need for better pay and other benefits. We get the impression that the police in the Imaginary City *are* organized (as the big salary increases during recent years would seem to suggest), but nobody seems to want to discuss the subject. Rex Burns's Denver policeman Gabriel Wager, on the other hand, has a great deal to say about the police union, most of it unfavorable. Lillian O'Donnell devotes much of the story of *No Business Being a Cop* to the problems of police unionism: Sergeant Norah Mulcahaney is not anti-union, but she is troubled by the possible impact of unionism on the professional aspects of police work.

Politics, especially partisan politics, is another subject that gets little attention in the 87th Precinct stories. There is some awareness of departmental politics, of course, but with nothing like the intensity of treatment in the procedurals of Lawrence Treat, whose Detective Mitch Taylor seems to be perpetually trapped in a miasma of departmental politics, or in those of Lawrence Sanders, whose Edward X. Delaney must expend almost as much of his energy on the politicians as on the perpetrators. Party politics is one of the themes developed by Dorothy Uhnak in *The Investigation*, where the involvement of the police in an upcoming mayoral election represents a situation foreign to the world of the 87th Precinct.

One other point of difference may serve to define McBain's special approach to the nature of the police sub-culture. Maj Sjöwall and Per Wahlöö, the Swedish procedural writers who often reveal the influence of McBain, make a strong point of the poor quality of people who are attracted into police work: they are recruited from those who do not attend a trade school or a university, they need only a D average to get into the police academy, and so on. The 87th Precinct cops do not make comments like these; instead, McBain dramatizes the dangers of poor quality in the person of Richard Genero, who became a detective only as a result of the merest chance and whose stupidity comes closer to the legendary level each time he appears. There are two things to be kept in mind here, both basic to the McBain technique. The first is that, typically, the problem of Genero and his kind is personified, individualized, so that Genero serves not only a social but a comic function, along with all the assorted nuts and oddballs that decorate the public of the 87th Precinct series. The other thing is that Genero came into his present position as successor to Bert Kling, who started out as young, green, and in many respects almost as dumb as Genero. Kling, though, has undergone the most remarkable growth and maturity of all the people in the story, a reminder that in police life, as in other forms of human endeavor, there are no stereotypes.

The refusal to stereotype, the insistence upon the distinctiveness of each individual in the story, is a conscious element of the McBain craftsmanship, which has also successfully resisted the temptation to fall into an easy formula. This refusal is amplified in his handling of the people who commit crimes and their victims, as we shall see in Chapter 6.

Chapter 6

Crime, Criminals, and Victims

In all likelihood, the people in the 87th Precinct are not too different from those in a corresponding area of Manhattan—or in any inner-city in this country—except for one thing. They are characters in mystery stories that are written for the same market as the books of P. D. James, Robert Parker, and John D. MacDonald. Because this is so, we must approach any discussion of them in the context of the traditions of mystery fiction, bearing in mind that the formulas and conventions of the mystery craft are bound to have a marked effect on their behavior, including the ways they murder, maim, and rob each other.

If we want to take a comprehensive look at the nature of criminals and victims in mystery fiction, the 87th Precinct saga offers a first-class opportunity, for the reason that the series has continued longer than any other of its type and has consequently produced accounts of a variety of crimes extended over a very respectable period.

Any approach to the study of crime and its effects in the 87th Precinct series must be conditioned by one special feature of these stories, which is shared by most police procedurals: they sometimes have a "modular" structure,[1] characterized by parallel plots representing the several cases on which the police detectives are working. One result of this kind of organization is that many of the novels will contain accounts of several crimes, often unrelated except by the fact that they are all part of the work-load of the same detectives.

Although a given policeman is probably involved in a half-dozen or more investigations at once (as Steve Carella complains on several occasions), a skillful narrator like Ed

McBain knows better than to scatter his story-telling efforts too broadly, but will focus our interest on the one or two mysteries that supply the material for the major plots. At the same time he will keep us reminded of the diverse nature of police work by furnishing quick glimpses into the other cases, as he does when he gives us one of those views of the squad room on a busy afternoon, crowded with prostitutes, shoplifters, and maybe even a murderer or two.

Because of certain significant differences between those two kinds of cases, besides the obvious difference in the amount of attention they receive, we will distinguish between them by the use of the designation of the main-plot stories as "primary" and the others as "incidental." These terms, of course, do not correspond to the familiar distinction between *major* and *minor* crimes; often the "incidental" crimes in the 87th Precinct stories are as serious as those in the main plots, like that brief account in *Hail, Hail, the Gang's All Here!* of the elderly woman who has just massacred all four members of her family. There may be, and often is, more than one primary case in a given novel, as in *Heat*, where the reader's attention is shared by the efforts of the police to solve the murder of Jeremiah Newman and by Jack Halloran's attempts to kill Bert Kling. The effect of the technique is to focus the attention of the reader on one or more of the mysteries to be solved and at the same time to keep him reminded of the world of crime just beyond the borders of the immediate story.

Because we are seeking as much information as possible about the nature of crime and its victims in the 87th Precinct, this chapter will be concerned almost exclusively with the primary cases, bearing in mind that they collectively represent only a selected fraction of the total.

The fundamental difference between fiction and fact becomes apparent when we compare the types of crimes treated in the stories with those in the world of non-fictional reality. Of all the primary crimes reported in the thirty-six 87th Precinct stories, fifty-six per cent are murders, about twenty-five per cent are cases of assault, and only eight per cent are cases of theft.[2] Compare this distribution with the one reported for New York City in the Department of Justice figures for 1980, where among non-narcotics cases murder accounts for only two-tenths of one per cent of the total, assault six per cent, and the various forms of theft ninety-two per cent.[3] The disparity is of course not surprising, because writers of mystery fiction select those episodes that will interest their readers, not necessarily those that represent a cross-section of the state of affairs in the "real" world. The police procedural, which belongs in the hard-boiled category of mystery fiction, is often characterized as "realistic," but those writers who want to retain their customers know better than to build their stories exclusively around the prosaic incidents to which real-life police detectives devote their time and attention.

Because murder is the theme of most of the 87th Precinct stories—as it usually is in detective fiction—we will examine the nature of this crime first and in some detail, together with its perpetrators and victims.

Sixty-five murderers have appeared in the stories to date, including the actual perpetrators and their accomplices. Of this number, fifty-six are men, and only nine are women. The distribution by ethnic background is fifty-nine non-Hispanic caucasians, five blacks, and one Puerto Rican.[4] For most of them no age is given, but among those whose ages we know, the largest number belong in the teen-age group and the second largest are in their thirties. Their occupations offer a significant insight into the nature of artistic selection in crime fiction: instead of a clustering of murderers in those walks of life with which policemen in the "mean streets" must deal, we have a tremendous range of professions and vocations that includes an actor, a worker in woodcrafts, and an attorney. Actually, only ten of the sixty-five can be classed as professional criminals, a group just slightly larger than the number of murderers from the respectable professions like engineering and nursing. The individual who single-handedly kills more people than any other murderer in the series is a quiet little fellow forty-seven years of age, whose occupation is not stated but who has an office in some kind of legitimate commercial enterprise downtown.

The 87th Precinct does come close to the non-fiction world in one respect. According to the Department of Justic report, fifty-one per cent of the murders in real life are committed by relatives or persons acquainted with their victims.[5] In the 87th

Precinct the proportion is forty-nine per cent of murders committed by persons who have at least a slight acquaintance with their victims. McBain does not keep it in the family to the extent that the real world does, however; only twelve per cent of his victims are killed by family members (including lovers), in comparison with sixteen per cent in non-fictional life.

A look at the tabulation of motives for murder in Appendix F shows that they are almost as varied as the social backgrounds of the murderers themselves, and they are additional evidence of the skillful hand of the narrative artist rather than any attempt at consistency with the real world. They range from such purely emotional motivations as jealousy and racial hatred to such rational ones as the desire to assume the identity of the victim. The most prevalent motive is the need to cover up another murder or some lesser crime, which causes almost a fourth of all the killings. This category includes parallel murders committed to establish a misleading pattern, the murder of a witness of an earlier crime, and a killing to prevent discovery of incriminating information. Here is an interesting contrast between the 87th Precinct stories and the classic tale of detection: in the novels and short stories of Agatha Christie, according to Earl Bargainnier, money is the overwhelmingly dominant motive.[6] In the 87th Precinct, however, there have been only three killings motivated strictly by financial gain, and to this point no one has murdered a parent, spouse, or other relative in order to inherit money. Six murders have been committed by persons of unsound mind who, under the M'Naughten Rule, could be found not guilty by reason of insanity.[7]

The weapons used by murderers in the stories come a little closer to real life than their motives do, but not much. Reference to the table in Appendix F will show that McBain's murders are committed with handguns less than a third of the time; in real murder cases, the proportion is fifty per cent. The murderers in the 87th Precinct stories use knives and razors in about the same proportion as do real-life killers; they kill with rifles more frequently than do the non-fictional murderers, but use shotguns far less frequently. They kill with the so-called "personal weapons" (hands, fists, feet) with more than twice the frequency of the murderers in the United States as a whole.[8]

In his choice of murder weapons, McBain stays reasonably close to non-fiction while maintaining enough variety to keep his audience attentive.

Among the victims of murder in the 87th Precinct, fifty-nine are men and thirty-three women. (The sex of the infant victim in *Hail to the Chief* is not given.) The ethnic breakdown is seventy-two non-Hispanic caucasians, fourteen blacks, and seven Puerto Ricans. A comparison with the Department of Justice report shows that McBain tends to favor the use of the white victim: in the country as a whole, in 1980, slightly more than half of the murder victims were white non-Hispanics, about forty per cent black, and nine per cent of Hispanic descent.[9] Actually, McBain tended for a long time to avoid murders involving ethnic minorities. One of the victims in *Cop Hater* was a black policeman, but there is not another black murder victim until the church bombing in *Hail, Hail, the Gang's All Here!* Likewise, there were two Puerto Rican victims in *The Pusher* and a Puerto Rican policeman killed in *See Them Die,* but not another one until *Hail to the Chief.* The ages of the victims in the 87th Precinct tend to be greater than those of their killers, clustering around the 20s, 30s, and 40s.

Earlier we mentioned the personal relationships between murderers and victims, whereby people tend to kill people they know, as in the case in real life. We can be a little more specific about actual family connections: wives kill husbands in the 87th Precinct at about the national rate (three per cent), but husbands kill wives twice as often as the U.S. as a whole. Lovers are also more lethal: five per cent of the victims in the 87th are killed by lovers, in comparison with three per cent in the whole country.[10]

As was the case among the murderers, there is no pattern in the distribution of occupations of the victims in the 87th Precinct. No single vocations seem to be especially susceptible to murder, not even blackmailers and burglars. There are only four professional criminals in the list of victims, about the same as the number of musicians. As we might expect in mystery stories, there is almost no relationshp between the occupations of the victims and the motives for their murders. For example, six policemen have been killed in the first thirty-six stories, but only one of these (Frankie Hernandez) died in line of duty. One was murdered by his wife and her lover, two others to establish a false pattern, one was killed as an innocent bystander (Haviland), and one as an indirect result of his involvement in a rakeoff operation. The same pattern (or absence of pattern) holds true in the cases of the three murdered prostitutes, none of whom was killed because of her profession. Actually, we find a positive relationship only among the four professional criminals, all of whom were murdered because they were criminals.[11] Generally, the absence of relationship between occupation and motive reminds us once again that we are dealing with the mystery story and that writers in this genre, whether of the classic or the hard-boiled school, tend to employ combinations that are surprising and unsuspected.

In one of the stories we are told that there is a strong correspondence between the time of year and frequency of crime. Warm weather brings criminals out like cockroaches, according to this statement, while the winter months, although much harder on the fire department, slow things down a little for the police.[12] As the table in Appendix F shows, though, the murderers in the 87th tend to prefer the pleasantest times of the year: October leads the other months in numbers of murders reported, closely followed by April. It is true that March and November have produced the smallest numbers of murders reported, but July and August are not far ahead of them.

The most frequent murder site in the 87th Precinct is the interior of an apartment, usually the victim's own. Not surprisingly, the next largest number of murders takes place in the street or alleyway. Aside from these norms, however, it is not easy to distinguish safe locales from unsafe ones: to date, more people have been killed in churches and synagogues than in whorehouses.

Assault is the second most frequent crime in the 87th Precinct stories, ranking far behind murder as the substance of the main plots. Under the heading of "assault" we will consider all those occasions on which one person physically attacks another or threatens another with a dangerous weapon, and also all cases of attempted murder.

There are some marked differences between the assailants and the murderers in the story, though there is, expectedly, a considerable overlap between the two groups. They are more heavily weighted on the male side than are the murderers; a greater proportion of them are of Puerto Rican descent, but they tend toward the same age-groups as the murderers.

There is considerably less diversity in the occupations of the assault perpetrators than there was with the murderers. It is not surprising that almost one-third of these people are professional criminals or members of street gangs. Among the rest, however, there is much the same randomness as might be found in any other type of mystery fiction: three cooks, one student, one accountant, and so on. Among individuals, one of the most dangerous assailants is a thirty-nine-year-old woman with an independent income.

The personal relationships between perpetrators of assault and their victims correspond much less to real life than was the case with the murderers and their victims, because only slightly more than one-fourth of the victims of assault are even slightly acquainted with their attackers. The disparity can be explained in part by the fact that more than half of the attacks are directed toward policemen, a phenomenon to which we will return shortly.

The most common site of assault in the 87th Precinct is the city street, which outnumbers the apartment by better than two to one. The single location of the largest incidence of assault is the detective squad room at precinct headquarters, but this circumstance is somewhat distorted by the fact that four cases of assault were perpetrated there by the same person on an October afternoon back in 1957.[13]

The motives for assault are not very different from those for murder, in that something like half of them involve a need to avoid arrest or to cover some other crime. Revenge is the next most common motive, followed by theft and extortion.

The handgun is used in assault with about the same frequency as in murder, a little less than thirty per cent of the time. The rifle and shotgun almost disappear from the list of the weapons used by the assailant, and so, curiously, does the knife, which among murderers in the 87th is second in popularity to the handgun. Hands, fists, and feet take a strong second place among assault weapons, being used in twenty-seven per cent of the cases.[14] Two assault weapons remind us once again that we are still in the world of mystery fiction: a surgeon's scalpel and a black widow spider.

There are thirty-seven primary cases of assault described in the stories, with male victims in twenty-nine of those and females is only eight. The proportion of male victims is considerably heavier than it is among murder victims, a disparity created at least in part by the fact that, of the twenty-nine cases of assault against men, nineteen are directed against policemen. The ethnic origins are similarly unbalanced, thirty-two of the victims being non-Hispanic caucasians, only three black and two Puerto Rican. They also tend to be young, with most of them in the 20s and 30s age-groups.

The large number of attacks upon policemen is another reminder of the dangerous nature of law enforcement as it is portrayed in the police procedural. Steve Carella has been shot twice, beaten six times, and badly burned once. The youthful Bert Kling was shot with a zip gun while still a patrolman and has since been beaten twice and shot at twice. Meyer Meyer was one of those pistol-whipped by Virginia Dodge in *Killer's Wedge,* was later beaten by a bunch of teen-agers and was most recently shot by a burglar resisting arrest. Cotton Hawes, another of Virginia Dodge's victims, has taken two other beatings, one embarrassingly administered by an extremely sexy young woman. The single-incident victims include detectives Arthur Brown (struck with a pistol) and Andy Parker (shot during a burglary), and uniformed policemen Alf Miscolo (shot and almost killed by Virginia Dodge) and Ronnie Fairchild (severely beaten by John Cacciatore). Of the nineteen attacks on policemen, twelve were cases of resisting or avoiding arrest; three were for purposes of revenge, two resulted from mistaken identity, one was committed as part of an extortion scheme, and one in the process of a robbery (Appendix G).

Murder and assault, as we said earlier, comprise more than four-fifths of all the primary cases in the 87th Precinct saga. There are, however, a few other crimes that also receive major narrative development.

The various forms of theft—including burglary, armed robbery, and confidence games—do not ordinarily provide such good story material as murder does, with the result that very few mystery novels have theft as their theme in spite of the fact that it is a far more prevalent crime than murder or assault. One feature of the nine primary cases of theft in the 87th Precinct that strikes us immediately is the broad spectrum of perpetrators, which includes one pair of seedy con men who prey upon visitors to the city, one elderly retired judge who stages an elaborate charade with imagined ghosts to cover his stealing from members of his own family, and a closet rapist, who steals only women's used underclothing. Actually, of the nine cases, three are unsuccessful attempts. A member of the 87th Squad breaks up the confidence racket when its perpetrators try to pull the pearl-switch on him; the series criminal, the notorious Deaf Man, foils the other two, once purposely when he stages a fake holdup to cover a real one, and once accidentally when he enters a shop for purposes of assassination and becomes involved in a shoot-out with a pair of thugs who are undertaking an armed robbery of the same premises.

Arson appears as a primary crime in two of the novels. It is one of the list of charges placed against the Deaf Man's accomplices at the end of *The Heckler,* when they have burned and blasted large sections of downtown Isola to cover a bank robbery. The other appearance is in *Bread,* in which Roger Grimm's warehouse and his home are deliberately burned in an effort at intimidation.

Of the four abductions in the series, only one is a genuine kidnapping for the collection of a ransom, the one in *King's Ransom.* Two are for purposes of sexual enslavement, one of a woman by a male (*So Long As You Both Shall Live*) and one of a man by a woman (*Calypso).* The other is the abduction of Detective Steve Carella in *Doll,* to find out how much information the police have on a murder.

In the breakdown of kinds of crimes in Appendix F we have counted only two of the thirty-five muggings in *The Mugger* (Katherine Elio and Eileen Burke), because the earlier instances do not really get into the story. Detective Burke, it should be noted, has had a bad record of experience with male police escorts: she is attacked again in *Ice* (this time by a would-be rapist) and narrowly escapes serious injury. In the one other mugging, in *Hail, Hail, the Gang's All Here* there are two perpetrators, a black woman and a white man.

In spite of the fact that they have become a major crime problem in real life, drugs have furnished the primary cases in only two novels (*The Pusher* and *Bread*). There was one case of marijuana possession in *Give the Boys a Great Big Hand,* but it involved only a trashy couple who were incidental to the main plot of the book. The drug traffic is very much in the picture in *Ice,* but only as background for the murder mysteries.

Blackmail and rape are featured once each. The blackmail attempt (by Mario Torressa against Lucy Mencken in *Killer's Payoff)* is foiled by the police, but the rape of a young woman in *Lady, Lady, I Did It!* results in a botched abortion and her subsequent death.[15]

When we turn to consideration of what we are calling "incidental" crimes in the series—those that get only brief treatment as background for the "primary" cases—we find very few data with regard to sex, ethnic backgrounds, or ages of the perpetrators or their victims, because the nature of their place in the narrative precludes much development of detail. There is, however, one significant difference between them, collectively, and the primary stories they supplement. This difference lies in the distribution of the types of crimes they represent.

Before we examine that difference, we should take a look at the artistic purposes these incidental episodes serve, which tend to be atmospheric rather than environmental, as in the accounts of the three shoplifters in *Sadie When She Died,* whose presence in the story supplies a part of the feel of Christmas as it is experienced by policemen in a big city. They may be used also for purposes of contrast, in order to sharpen the effect of the major plot of a story, as they pointedly do in *Jigsaw,* where three brief accounts of crimes based on the most primitive of motives are tucked into the narrative in such manner as to invite comparison with the complexity of involvements in the jigsaw puzzle the police are trying to solve. Occasionally, they are illustrations of the frantic pressures of police work, where there is always more to do than the squad can possibly handle; this is the situation in *Let's Hear It for the Deaf Man,* at that point when the detectives of the 87th have just realized that they are about to experience another confrontation with their old foe the Deaf Man, while they are trying to deal simultaneously with a man who has been brought into the squad room with an arrow in his chest, a screaming woman in the detention cage who has slashed her boy friend, two badly stoned teen-agers who have been nabbed for stealing a Cadillac, and an elderly lady whose purse has been snatched. It is not unusual for mystery stories, especially those in the field of police fiction, to be full of references to or hints at large numbers of crimes besides those under investigation in the immediate account, but McBain's skill in using them to supplement his main plots is remarkable.

It is not surprising, then, that the crimes recounted in these subordinate episodes tend to be less dramatic than those in the main plots. Murder figures far less prominently, occurring in only nineteen per cent of them, in comparison with fifty-six per cent in the primary ones. The proportion of cases of assault, on the other hand, is about the same as in the main plots. The crime that shows up most frequently in the incidental episodes is theft, which thirty-five per cent of them involve, and which, as we explained earlier, is closer to the distribution of crimes in New York City, as reported by the Department of Justice for 1980.[16] Whether by design or not, the writer has suggested a world of crime, just outside the main interests of the novels themselves, in which the kinds of problems with which the police must deal are more like those in the non-fictional world than are those at the center of the mystery story.

One generalization almost inevitable from the data regarding crime in the 87th Precinct is that Ed McBain has kept his narrative within the mainstream of the mystery tradition. Certainly one indication of the authority of convention in the series lies in the fact that, regardless of inventions and side-issues, the main theme of every one of the thirty-six novels is murder or the threat of murder, as it has been in the detective novel from Conan Doyle to the present.

The reason most mystery novelists write exclusively about murder is not that it is the crime with which the detectives must deal most often; as we have seen earlier, the reverse is true, with murders accounting for a negligible fraction of crimes, especially in comparison with such offenses as theft and narcotics dealing, which are really epidemic in contemporary society. The reason mystery writers write about murder is that it is the most extreme of all human acts, and the most naturally dramatic. The convention of the murder-plot was so well established fifty years ago that S.S. Van Dine could insist, as one of his "Twenty Rules," that no other crime was worth a reader's making his way through a book-length mystery.[17] The tradition was continued by writers like Dashiell Hammett and Raymond Chandler, who might start their plots with investigation of some lesser mystery like that of a missing person, but must inevitably turn to the resolution of one or more murders during the story.

If further confirmation of Ed McBain's place in the tradition of the mystery story is needed, it can be discovered by attention to the material with which he deals, which would include the people in his stories, both perpetrators ard victims, their occupations, their motives, and the circumstances under which they offend or are offended against. The total effect places McBain's Imaginary City much closer to the New York of the Nero Wolfe stories than to the New York of this evening's news. It may be that this firm grounding in a durable tradition is one reason why the 87th Precinct series has continued to flourish while others, more topical and contemporary, have disappeared.

Chapter 7

Steve Carella

The 87th Precinct series has come closer than any other to realization of the police procedural ideal of the group protagonist, of team effort accomplishing the results in detection that had been achieved in the older traditional mystery by the efforts of one brilliant individual like Sherlock Holmes or Miss Marple. Most writers have at least recognized that in real life most crimes are cleared up through the joint efforts of a number of police detectives rather than those of a single hero, but few of them have been able to achieve anything like full realization, because the conventions of popular fiction tend to over-ride those of realism, and heroes emerge almost automatically; thus we speak of the George Gideon stories of J.J. Marric and the Norah Mulcahaney stories of Lillian O'Donnell, in spite of the fact that both of those are procedural series celebrated for their plausible representation of police life. Maj Sjowall and Per Wahloo almost achieved a corporate hero in the stories about the Stockholm police, but even those are habitually called the Martin Beck series. Nobody, though, ever speaks of "the Steve Carella stories."

Actually, Ed McBain had intended to adhere even more closely to the premise of a "conglomerate protagonist," as he calls it, with the squad as hero and no individual in the spotlight. In the earliest stories, he was developing a plan that would keep the cast of characters rotating; after all, in real life policemen retire, die in line of duty, or find other jobs. Consequently, McBain killed off three of his detectives in the first book in the series, and then killed Steve Carella at the end of *The Pusher*. Carella stayed dead, as McBain explains, just long enough for his editor to read through the manuscript, then to call back and say, "You can't kill Carella. He's the hero. He's the star of the series."[1] Thus Public Opinion intervened (in the person of Herb Alexander), Carella recovered from his gunshot wound, and the death-rate among cops in the 87th dropped drastically.

The change in Carella's role is one thing that must be kept in mind in understanding him as a fictional character. Once rescued from death, he apparently took on a special identity in the mind of Ed McBain, to the extent that he has become a criterion and occasionally a spokesman.

Which brings us to the other special quality of Carella's place in the series: he sometimes not only speaks for his author but tends to share his attitudes and opinions.[2] His role as interpreter becomes most easily apparent in his love-hate relationship with the City, especially in those passages like the one in *The Con Man*, where he glories in it, or the one in *Long Time No See*, where he despairs of it. There are other times when Carella seems to act only as a voice, as when he wonders aloud why it is that we expect everything to go right just because we have been able to put men on the moon.

We know more about Carella's family background and his early history than those of any of the rest of the squad, though the story must be gleaned in snatches from all over the series. Steve is a third-generation American, his grandfather having migrated from Naples to the City, where he drove a milk wagon. The older Carellas seem to have had their share of insecurities, believing for example that dreams are omens of things to come, and stuffing the kids with family horror stories like the one about Uncle Charlie who accidentally blinded himself in one eye while trimming his eyebrows and Uncle Salvatore who slipped on the ice and was thenceforth confined to a wheelchair. Steve was born in Isola, the son of Antonio (a baker) and Louisa Carella, but the family moved to Riverhead while he was still a child. Two sensations from his boyhood continue to visit Carella in adulthood: the memory of sitting on a grassy hilltop on his aunt's farm in the next state, and of his mother calling "Stevie! Supper!" from the upstairs window of their family home on a quiet evening in April. Steve's relationship with his sister Angela seems to have been remarkably wholesome, to the extent that even on her wedding day she insists on confiding some intimate details to him rather than to their mother. In some respects Steve's boyhood seems to have been rather tightly insulated, but his associations with those of his own religious persuasion were close, to the extent of his having his first carnal knowledge of one Suzie Ryan, a good Irish lass, on the roof of an apartment building when he was fifteen.

Steve was in the infantry during World War II and served in Italy, where he was wounded by a hand grenade. He managed to get two and a half years of college, dropping out, according to his own account, when "Chaucer finally threw me." No further details of this educational crisis are available, and the reader may have reason to suspect that Chaucer was more an excuse, or maybe a last straw, than a catastrophe. The only other details we know from Carella's pre-*Cop Hater* existence are his joining the police force at the age of twenty-one and his sending Frank Dodge to Castleview Penitentiary in September 1953.

When Carella's physical appearance is described, as it is more often than that of anybody else, two qualities are inevitably mentioned. We are always told about his lithe muscularity, his strength that is more graceful than brawny. The other feature is, of course, his eyes, always represented as slanting downward, giving him a slightly Oriental look (attributed once, remarkably, to Arab incursions into his ancestral Sicily) and especially giving him a mildly mournful look that belies his basically optimistic makeup. The outward appearance is the key to the inner man: Steve Carella, strong and competent, basically well-adjusted and untroubled, is capable of genuine sorrow.

Carella's strength, as a detective and as a fictional character, is his ability to get along with people. In this respect he is considerably above average, comparing favorably with such good cops as Hillary Waugh's Fred Fellows, who is exemplary in personal relationships, and ranking even with such a paragon as John Ball's Virgil Tibbs. Carella's basic humanity comes into evidence early in *Cop Hater*, where he is courteous to a suspect in contrast to Bush's roughness, and as the series progresses this consideration for others continues virtually unchanged. One key to his ability to work with people is his trick of getting out from under the stresses of the job when he goes home. At that point in *Killer's Choice* when Cotton Hawes, whose arrogance has already alienated him from his squad, almost causes Steve's death by a stupid miscalculation, Carella is the only person who does not discuss the situation at home, being so wrapped up (literally) in his beautiful Teddy that the anxieties of his job are far removed from his consciousness.

Part of his success in dealing with civilians is his judgment of when to be considerate and when to be firm. He is habitually **considerate** of older people, to the extent of taking time during a busy investigation to spend a few extra minutes with an old man who is obviously lonely. With people who do not understand English he can speak Spanish or Italian. He consciously avoids stereotyping, refusing, for example, to categorize young people as "freaks." At the same time Carella is capable of firmness with snobs and phonies, like the producer Alan Carter in *Ice*, whose presumptiousness he deflates with a single quick thrust. He also knows how to deal firmly with more honest people who undertake to stereotype him, as he does with Sophie Harris in *Long Time No See*, when she tries to evade the truth by resort to a racist position.

There have been a few people whom Steve despises and with whom he finds it impossible to deal with his usual equanimity. Foremost among these, undoubtedly, is Cliff Savage, the newspaper reporter whose eagerness for a story comes close to causing Teddy's death in *Cop Hater*; Carella never forgives Savage, though he does later tone down his vengeful feelings. Another is Douglas King in *King's Ransom*, who refuses to pay the ransom for the son of his faithful chauffeur. Then there is Harry Caine, the recording producer who has been consistently cheating the artists in *Calypso*; Carella's revlusion is so strong that after interviewing him he goes out into the rain to find a patrolman to ticket Caine's car.

Carella finds it a problem to establish a relationship with certain people because they give him the willies. This is frequently the case with women, especially older women and more especially grieving women and those who begin to weep in his presence. People without moral scruples make him uncomfortable, like Mrs. Thomlinson in *Like Love*, who condones her daughter's adultery.

Carella's relationship with his fellow policemen is considerably above average for a cop in fiction. With the inevitable pair from Homicide he can always hold his own, exchanging insults and obscenities both joking and corrosive, playing the game with exaggerated courtesy and consideration for delicate feelings. With the assistant medical examiner, on the other hand, he is always tactful, and he consequently seems to be the only man on the squad capable of dealing effectively with the petulant Blaney.

His professionalism is most clearly seen in his attitude toward Ollie Weeks. Ollie is scorned by the rest of the squad because he is bigoted and is crude in speech and maner, and he stinks (physically). Steve is the only member of the team who can caution Ollie about his behavior, because he recognizes that, in spite of his unappetizing presence, Ollie is a good cop.

Steve is most comfortable with Meyer, with whom his relationship is customarily expressed in their ability to joke with each other. With Hawes he is usually more serious, inclined toward discussion of books and movies. Toward Kling he seems to feel a special responsibility, to the extent that he takes it upon himself to try to rehabilitate him in *Doll* (when nobody else can stand to have him around), steadies him with personal advice during Augusta's abduction, and finally, when Kling is prostrate over Gussie's adultery, it is Steve who sits beside him and says simply, "Tell me."

Carella's association with Lieutenant Peter Byrnes is a son-to-father relationship that has part of its foundation in Byrnes's gratitude to him for his help in saving the lieutenant's son Larry from the frame in *The Pusher* and partly in his awareness of Steve as the backbone of the squad. Byrne does not hesitate to caution Carella about his tendency to hold grudges against people like Cliff Savage, but neither does he hestitate to ask Carella to come back on duty in an emergency, even when Steve needs rest from his own long shift.

The one fellow cop Carella can not stand is Andy Parker, in which attitude he is part of the unanimous opinion of the squad. Parker is the only other cop with whom Carella has a fist fight (in *Give the Boys a Great Big Hand*), significantly because Parker insists on picking on Frankie Hernandez until the business goes beyond Steve's endurance.

At the same time, Carella's habitual kindness extends itself to the other people on the squad, even poor dumb Genero, whom he treats courteously when they are both in the hospital and Genero is obviously digging him for a promotion.

Toward policemen of inferior rank he exhibits the same combination of consideration and firmness as with civilians. He feels like a heel when his jumping a traffic light prompts a rain-soaked patrolman to yell at him, but he does not hesitate to chase the patrolmen out of the squad room where they have congregated to gawk at the sexy Helen Vale.

Carella comes as close as any detective in police procedural fiction to realization of the ideal of professionalism; he is not as dogmatic as John Ball's Jack Tallon, or as aggressively professional as Lillian O'Donnel's Norah Mulcahaney, but overall he measures up well in comparison to most of the others. He takes his work seriously: "I just do my job," he tells Meyer, when Meyer tries to joke with him about the fictional triad of Motive, Means, and Opportunity. Unlike just about everybody else, Carella never drinks at lunch while on duty. Who else would tell a civilian, "Think of me as a priest," as he does when Roger Grimm hesitates to allow him access to the company's books, and when Heidi Beck hesitates to confide to him some intimate details about the murdered Muriel Stark? It works in both instances; people seem willing to share confidences with him because he does treat such matters with almost priestly seriousness. It seems only appropriate that Steve is the one called upon to go into the hideout of Pepe Miranda in *See Them Die* disguised as a priest.

Basically, Carella is an intuitive rather than a rationalistic detective. His approach to analysis is usually physical, in that he puts himself into situations and tries to feel possibilities. This is how he works out the problem of that locked door in *Killer's Wedge* and how he sees through the Deaf Man's double exposure ploy in *Let's Hear It for the Deaf Man*. He is quite capable of such sudden insights as the one he gains when, listening to Mrs. Wechsler's pronunciation, he realizes what her husband meant by "carpenter," but most of his successes are the result of resolute method.

In addition to these three successful resolutions, Carella

has shown up well in the recovery of the kidnapped boy in *King's Ransom*, in working out the complicated identity problem in *The Empty Hours*, in discerning what caused the death of Sarah Fletcher in *Sadie When She Died*, and in getting at the real motive behind the murders of the three blind beggers in *Long Time No See*. His results have been somewhat less than satisfactory in *The Pusher* (where he is shot in the chest), *The Heckler* (where the Deaf Man fills him with buckshot), *Doll* (where he spends most of the investigation handcuffed to a radiator), and *Fuzz* (where his only real distinction lies in his not looking any more stupid than the others on the squad).

Steve Carella does hold one unchallenged record, of having been wounded and otherwise injured in line of duty more often than any other member of the 87th Squad. He has been given up for dead three times (in *The Pusher, The Heckler,* and *Doll*) and otherwise hospitalized for beatings, burns, and involuntary heroin injections. To date there have been five occasions on which he has received first aid treatment for injuries inflicted by suspects or by friends of victims, and by some minions of the Deaf Man, who embarrassingly mugged and robbed him (Appendix G).

We should say a special word about Carella's relationship with the Deaf Man, which comes close to being unique in police fiction. These two are mortal enemies, each having once shot the other, but Carella tells himself that he has stopped thinking of the Deaf Man as a deadly adversary, and when the Deaf Man calls the squad room to taunt him for the failure of the police to see through the double-clue challenge, Carella boldly returns the bluff as if he were dealing with one of his friendly antagonists in another department. Significantly, though, Carella tends to identify the Deaf Man with his wife Teddy, who is also deaf, and he considers it ironic that the person he loves most and the one he fears most have the same affliction. This, as we will shortly see, is not the only time Carella identifies Teddy with somebody else.

Steve's cultural level is above that of most police detectives. With Cotton Hawes he can carry on a reasonably well-informed discussion of a movie, and in spite of his alleged difficulties with Chaucer he on one occasion quotes a fairly obscure passage from *Macbeth* (almost accurately), citing act *and* scene,[3] and at another time a phrase from Joyce's *Ulysses* crosses his mind. His attitude toward mystery fiction is paradoxical: at one point he is an inveterate murder-mystery reader but at another a hater of mysteries who turns off the TV when a cop show comes on. All the same, his conversational allusions reveal a familiarity with *Dragnet*, as well as the works of Agatha Christie, Ross Macdonald, and John Dickson Carr.

His taste in humor also displays some contradictions. He winces at the cutesy name "Grimports" for Roger Grimm's import business and at Ollie Week's calling him "Steve-a-reeno," but he is capable of a godawful pun like "the dread Scott decision." Steve's sense of humor is generally conventional, of the type that might be absorbed from watching Stan Gifford (of *Eighty Million Eyes*) and other such TV comics.

The long-range changes in Carella's emotional makeup are usually indicators of how things are going at home. We become aware of one of the slumps in spirit early in the series: he jokes cheerfully with Meyer in *Lady Killer*, makes that one bad pun in *Killer's Wedge*, is quite serious through *'Til Death*, then becomes grim and irritable in *King's Ransom*. The change is perfectly logical, of course, from a man experiencing his wife's first pregnancy (including some worry about whether the child may inherit its mother's deafness), the unexpected birth of twins and the consequent severe financial strain. After things improve, though, he is reasonably cheerful until the period of *Long Time No See*, when he begins to feel the lack of professional advancement, and he continues quite somber in *Calypso*, declining to join in laughter at Meyer's joke and offering no humor of his own.

Steve Carella's marriage has been the most successful one to date in the whole police procedural canon, his relations with Teddy coming as close to the idyllic as is possible in contemporary fiction. That marriage has been tested by financial disasters after the birth of the twins (but almost miraculously rescued by the altruistic Fanny, who has stayed on as nurse and general housekeeper for her room and keep), and it is occasionally strained by Teddy's susceptibility to attacks of depression because of her deafness and the prospective loss of youth and beauty. In reply to Bert Kling's question of whether their marriage is still good "in bed," though, Carella answers, "Yes ... And everywhere else." Steve is subject to such male shortcomings as forgetting to buy Teddy a Valentine present, but he means it when he tells her, "I love you more than life." His relations with the twins have suffered less tension than those with Teddy. Like any normal father he takes them trick-or-treating, and he even buys a rhyming dictionary to keep a promise to his daughter April to make up a poem about her.

A few paragraphs back we mentioned Carella's habit of identifying Teddy's deafness with that of the Deaf Man, usually in a context of the hate-fear contrast of which he is so frequently reminded. The identification-projection of Teddy is even more pointed in *Ghosts*, where he is struck by the resemblance of the Scott twins to her, and the similarity takes on a supernatural effect when Hillary, the psychic one, knows about it without having seen Teddy. This projection seems to assume another dimension too in the involvement of the twins. McBain has never tended toward psychological complexity in the development of his characters, but Steve's repeated tendency to project Teddy into dramatic situations is too pointed to lack significance.

The dominant quality in Steve Carella's makeup is a powerful conscience, laced with a strong sense of guilt. It conditions his professional attitudes, as manifested by his refusal to drink on duty and to accept favors. It comes through with special strength, though, in his responses to those highly sexed women who are attracted to him, beginning with Alice Bush in *Cop Hater* and recurring with increasing frequency as he grows older. His first reaction to one of these brushes is to feel guilty, although he is never at fault, and then he is faced with the real problem: should he tell Teddy? Almost always he does, and almost always Teddy blazes up briefly in mute rage, but the storm subsides as quickly as it arises.

There are two things about Teddy Carella that people notice immediately. The first is her almost incredible beauty; as Alexander Pike, the photographer at Bert Kling's wedding, watches her dancing with Steve, he is fascinated by her black hair and by her eyes that are so brown they seem black too. The other is her adoration of her husband; when Roger Broome watches her alight from a taxi and join Steve downtown the one impression he has is that she is happy to be with this man. People are almost never aware of her total deafness right away because it is eclipsed by her quick intelligence.

Teddy comes close to being the idealized dream-mate, in the sense that her whole life is bound up in her husband, to the extent that her desire for him is almost obsessive, taking priority over even her feelings for her children. The predilection becomes apparent in one of those several blazing love scenes when she finds herself alone with Steve at the end of the day; his question, "Where are the children?" gets a quick dismissal, followed by the passionate commitment between husband and wife. The same predisposition is apparent in a scene in a later story, when April is getting her mother's help with some spelling. The closeness between mother and daughter dissolves the instant Carella arrives home from work.

Undoubtedly a large part of Teddy's emotional dependence on Steve is the result of insecurity growing out of her deafness. She is intensely anxious about the way people feel about her, and her anxiety about Steve's feelings for her produces those intense attacks of jealousy over his associations with other women and also her dread of the prospect of losing her own physical attractiveness. In a sense, Teddy personifies the twentieth century American obsession with youth and good looks, and our anxiety over the loss of sexual desirability.

At the same time, Teddy Carella is a person of considerable courage. It was she, we remember, who single-handedly tailed the murderous con man and his prospective victim right into his apartment, fully aware of the extreme danger to herself. Even more, though, she is a person of great moral courage, who refuses to let her handicap come between her and the enjoyment of life or her participation in the life of her husband.

Chapter 8

Meyer Meyer

Whatever else may be said of Meyer Meyer, he is unquestionably the best-tagged member of the 87th Squad, with no less than four solid identifications: 1. He is the one with the replicated name. 2. He is a Jew. 3. He is bald. 4. His age is, and always has been, thirty-seven. The first three of these are functionally related, and it is possible that the fourth is also.

Meyer tells Bert Kling that he is descended from a line of scholars, his grandfather being the only man in his town in Poland who could read and write. This was the grandfather who migrated to the City, and he was the father of Max Meyer, whose reputation as a comedian is still remembered by his contemporaries. We need not repeat the account of the naming of young Meyer, because it is the most frequently recounted story in the series, appearing in full almost as often as Meyer himself appears. About his mother we know very little, except that Meyer in adulthood tends to identify with her in his dislike of hospitals and doctors (she died of cancer in a hospital) and in his habit of cursing in pig latin (she did not allow swearing in the house). Toward his father Meyer tends to feel a sense of shame (especially in regard to old Max's addiction to comedy), though he does sometimes share his father's values in feeling some guilt over owning a Mercedes and eating ham sandwiches.

Meyer was born in Riverhead, and as an Orthodox Jew in a predominantly Gentile neighborhood was the natural target of his frolicksome school mates who loved to chase him down the street yelling, "Meyer Meyer, Jew on fire!" threatening to burn him at the stake, and then beating the hell out of him.

Outnumbered by his Christian contemporaries, Meyer learned a patience that, as Strickland says, "makes Job look like a hyperactive jackrabbit."[1] The patience stays with Meyer through life, but the martyrdom ended when, at the age of sixteen, he weighed 190 pounds and was almost six feet tall. This was only a short time after Meyer had broken the tyranny over him of one Patrick Cassidy, one of his fun-loving companions who was determined to force Meyer to signify subservience with the traditional kiss, but Meyer instead seized the initiative in such a fashion that Cassidy (who is now a cop) can not sit down today without resting his anatomy on the scars of Meyer's tooth-marks.

Meyer attended law school, received his degree and passed the bar exam in 1940 but never had a chance to practice because he was immediately drafted into the Army. After discharge he decided the profession of law was not for him, so joined the police force and shortly thereafter married his college sweetheart, Sarah Lipkin. Meyer's patience saw him through the eight years that passed before he made Detective 3rd/Grade.

It is not possible to be completely confident about the account of Meyer's early life, because the details have tended to change. When the "Jew on fire" story appears in *Lady Killer* and some of the other early ones, the Gentile kids never carry out their threat to burn Meyer at the stake, but in *Hail to the Chief* (and again in *Long Time No See*) he remembers how it was only a providential rainstorm that put out the flames set by the young goyim around his feet. The same kind of slippage takes place in the story about his law training: in *Killer's Wedge*, Meyer receives his degree and passes his bar exams before being drafted, but in *Calypso* Patrick Cassidy (he who bears the scars of Meyer's teeth) talks him into quitting law school and becoming a cop.

If we were dealing with matters of great subtlety here, we might find it profitable to inquire the reason for Meyer's increasing tendency to place responsibility on the shoulders of his youthful companions. Following the practice of some of our more gifted critics, we could rather quickly identify a few crises like the murder of the Rabbi in *"J"* or Meyer's confrontation with Ludwig Etterman in *Ten Plus One* as symptoms of a growing paranoia, but the simple fact is that Meyer, who has been thirty-seven for more than a quarter of a century, is nevertheless growing older, and is apparently succumbing to the inclination of old age to embellish a good story. At any rate, it is worth noting that Meyer's sense of martyrdom increases with the re-tellings, suggesting that his consciousness of incipient paranoia may have some basis in fact.

One reason for never suspecting Meyer of any emotional hangups is the fact that he is married to one of the most stable people in the series. Sarah believes in a well-ordered household, where 1. the children eat what is put before them, including their green beans, 2. Meyer does not upset dinner by discussions of the seamy cases he is dealing with, and 3. the obligations of the family are observed, including attendance at the bar mitzvah and later the wedding of her nephew, Irwin the Vermin. Sarah is at her best when she furnishes a counterbalance for Meyer's upsets, as she does when he tries to torment himself over his own ambivalent status as a Jew in modern America; Sarah asks, "Shall I get your prayer shawl?" Meyer mutters "Wise guy," but the crisis is past.

In general, Meyer's relations with his fellow cops are good. One thing working in his favor is his sense of humor, which permits him to go along with a gag, as he does when Miscolo pretends the wino in the squad room is Meyer's father, but he knows enough to stop when somebody else is about to take offense. His attitude toward the shortcomings of his colleagues is one of cynical stoicism (as when Cotton Hawes' stupid blunder almost gets Carella killed), but he is capable of the strongest feelings for his close friends, and when the news of Carella's supposed death comes to the squad room in *Doll*, Meyer walks over to Grover Park, sits on a bench alone, and quietly weeps for his friend. Toward the uniformed branch his actions are considerate but firm: when a traffic cop bawls him out for blocking the street Meyer apologizes, but when an overzealous patrolman ruins his chance to catch the sniper in *Ten Plus One* red-handed, Meyer bawls him out with a threat to consign him to a beat in Bethtown.

Like most detectives in mystery fiction, Meyer likes to think of himself as a cool rationalist, but, also like most of them, he works most succesfully from instinct and intuition.

Early in the investigation of the Browser Bookstore massacre he is on the right track, rejecting the madman theory on the basis of feel alone. At one point in the sniper case he showers an acquaintance with elementary logic ("All men are bipeds, therefore all bipeds are men"), but then he is on much firmer ground during the Stan Gifford case when he refuses to accept suicide as a solution: "I don't like the feel." Meyer is really at his best, though, when he combines this feel for things with his common sense and his capacity for patient investigation, as he does when he learns how Steve Carella left the Sachs apartment carrying a doll and thus discovers a hitherto unsuspected connection.

He uses the same combination of abilities in his biggest single-handed success, the solution of the infestation of ghosts in the Gorman home in Smoke Rise. In that one, by the way, Meyer exhibits another quality that makes him an admirable cop: having unearthed a painful family secret, he lets the matter drop. Meyer's other outstanding triumph, though not strictly detectival in nature, comes when he and Miscolo successfully deliver the hooker's baby in the squad room in *Ice*. He provides valuable assistance, from his knowledge of Jewish lore, in the murder of Rabbi Soloman, and less consciously in the Stan Gifford murder, in the business of the time-release capsules. Meyer has only one real failure to his credit, his unsuccessful attempt to get help when the squad was being held by Virginia Dodge, but that was more the result of rotten luck than any serious miscalculation on Meyer's part.

In his professional dealings with the civilian world, Meyer is usually governed by his legendary patience, to the extent that he will stay at least outwardly cool during the extended questioning of an impeditive victim or witness. He is capable of warm sympathy, such as he feels for Reynolds after the kidnapping of his son in *King's Ransom*, or toward Tinka Sachs, when he observes that her murderer took two lives, the one she was ending as an addict and the one she was beginning as a convalescent (*Doll*). Toward pompous people and fakes, Meyer does not hesitate to apply the devastating squelch, of which he is a master. Dealing with petty criminals, his patience carries him up to the point at which the subject begins to lie to him or joke with him, whereupon he is capable of administering a slap or a kick in the pants. His old-fashioned sense of virtue comes to the fore when he pulls down the skirt of Oona Blake after having rendered her unconscious in *'Til Death*, and again when he decides he does not like Major Tataglia in *Long Time No See* because the major wears cologne.

Meyer's general adjustment to life is harder to summarize, not so much because of any deep currents within his psyche as because of the contradictions in his nature. He is not as sensitive about his name as Carella is, declining to correct somebody who calls him "Detective Breyer," but when Helen Hudson's novel *Meyer Meyer* appears, he is beside himself over the violation of his identity and threatens to sue. For many years he adopted an air of stoicism with regard to his baldness, but a head-consciousness begins to show up in *Calypso*, where he is wearing a Professor Higgins hat, then in *Ghosts*, where it is a deerstalker; in *Heat* he talks about buying a hairpiece, and in *Ice* he displays the watch cap Sarah knitted for him as a Valentine's Day gift. One other tendency in Meyer that may be symptomatic is his susceptibility to colds, which is more acute than that of anybody else on the squad.

One quality of Meyer that usually catches people's attention is his skill with humor. On one occasion Bert Kling praises Meyer's ability to tell a joke, and undoubtedly many of his jokes are passed on by readers as the things they remember in the books, like the one about the lady in Bethtown and the pink-nosed puppies, or the one about the rudeness of people in the City. Meyer's real talent, though, is with the running gag and the situational ad-lib, which are funnier than his formal jokes. He will keep something going like the cat-stealer in *The Mugger* or the bald eagle in *Doll* as long as his audience will tolerate it, or he can make one of those quick ironic jabs like his comment in *Like Love*, when he and Carella are making an inventory of the contents of a medicine cabinet, that such a listing in a book by J.D. Salinger would be considered a literary achievement. Sometimes, as a matter of fact, it is not easy to tell when Meyer is joking: is he serious when his friends accuse him of being a "closet goy" and he replies that he is really a closet Jew?

It may be that Meyer is inclined to the role of the

stereotyped Jewish comedian but is restrained by the memory of his father, whose talent was apparently irrepressible. At the conclusion of *The Heckler* he calls Dave Raskin pretending to be the Deaf Man renewing his campaign of harassment. Raskin catches on, chuckles, and tells Meyer he is just like his father. Meyer (who has lived a life of patient discomfort as a result of old Max's ebullience) suddenly feels a little ill.

It would be more accurate to say that Meyer's sense of humor is a reflection of a balanced outlook that gives him perspective on a great many things, including his own ethnic status. He has not been inside a synagogue in twenty years, we are told in an early story, and he demands butter for dinner despite Sarah's accusation that he is a heathen. Outwardly, Meyer makes a show of neutrality, celebrating both Chanukah and Christmas. Although he will not practice his ethnic heritage, he tends to fall back on it in a crisis. He still experiences identity as a Jew, in his tendency to "feel funny" around Germans and his ability to translate Hebrew. There is, moreover, in Meyer's background a kind of ethnic elitism that can effectively slam the door in the face of outsiders, as when Bert Kling wishes him *mazeltov*. "Gesundheit," replies Meyer.

Chapter 9

Bert Kling

The happy marriage of Steve Carella and the stable home life of Meyer Meyer are so closely woven into the stories of their detective careers as to be a natural part of the background. With Bert Kling, though, we have what amounts to two histories, a love-life plagued by hard luck and mischance, paralleled by a quite respectable career as a policeman.

We know almost nothing of Kling's life before that point at which he shows up as a uniformed patrolman in *Cop Hater*, except that as a youth he had lived in Riverhead and that he was a veteran of Korea. Both of his parents are dead at the time of his marriage to Augusta Blair.

Those aspects of Bert Kling with which we are familiar, though, reveal a personality characterized by sharp contrasts, especially that remarkable combination of innocence and maturity that has been with him from the beginning.

Innocent is the term that attaches itself to Kling when he first follows Carella around the whorehouses on Mason Avenue, gasping in astonishment at Steve's ease in handling the hardened madams. The label stays fixed during his free-lance investigation of the murder of Jeanne Paige in *The Mugger,* and it almost smothers him during his humiliation at the hands of the homicide cops and the coroner in *The Pusher.* His innocent demeanor, coupled with his boyish good looks, continue for a long time to elicit judgments like "a little young to be a detective," to the extent that even as late as *Calypso* he is still being called the "youngest detective on the squad," in spite of the fact that Genero had taken over that spot many years earlier; there is something about Kling that continues to give the impression of juniority.

All the same, Bert Kling has demonstrated a remarkable capacity for maturity since very early in his career with the 87th Squad. On their first date he forces Claire Townsend to reorganize that part of her emotional life that has been destroyed by the death of her boyfriend, and he handles five-year-old Monica Boone in *Killer's Choice* far better than anybody else on the squad could have. He is at his insightful best when he tries to reason with Virginia Dodge, and in spite of her calling him "sonny," Kling pronounces an apt judgment on her condition: "I should have known a person can't talk to a corpse."

The other contrast in Kling's makeup, which seems to be related to this mixture of innocence and maturity, is the contradictory combination of his capacity for independence in professional operation with that almost obsessive dependence upon the love of women.

On three separate occasions Kling embarks upon the undertaking so hazardous to the career of a policeman, the job of independent detection. First, recovering from his gunshot wound in *The Mugger,* he sets out to solve the Paige murder, partly as a result of the urging of an old school chum but mainly because he is ambitious for promotion to the detective squad; he succeeds where the regulars have failed, but only after a collision with a homicide lieutenant almost gets him fired from the force. Again in *Doll* he goes ahead in spite of the fact that Byrnes has pulled him off the Sachs case, and this time it is his quickness with his gun that saves Steve Carella's life. Then in *Heat,* with completely personal motives, he undertakes to find out whether Augusta is having an affair with a photographer, this time jeopardizing his future by falsifying information on an application for a search warrant. In each of these cases Kling is completely independent of any help from his fellow policemen.

In contrast to this independent spirit is that singular dependence of Bert Kling upon the love of women, of which we shall have more to say shortly.

In spite of his alleged juvenility, Kling is a good detective with a capacity for perceptiveness that borders on brilliance. In *The Con Man* it is he who sees through the significance of the call from Charlie Chen, in spite of the dense obtuseness of

Haviland. In *The Heckler,* Kling (partly as a result of his recent reading of "The Red-Headed League") sees the real direction of the Deaf Man's plan. He is also careful: in Cindy Forrest's bedroom after the attack on her he finds a little wad of earth that he passes on to the lab, and this piece of evidence eventually takes him to Cindy's assailant.

Kling's record of success is as good as that of anybody else on the squad. Besides those key roles in *The Mugger, Doll,* and *Eighty Million Eyes,* he has to his credit the apprehension of Al Brice in *Sadie When She Died* and the solution of the Kitten Burglar epidemic in *Let's Hear It for the Deaf Man.* Carella pays Bert's record a real tribute when he comments on the impossibility of finding Augusta's kidnapper among Kling's former arrestees: "He's sent up too many to count."

Except for that bad stretch of a few years following the death of Claire Townsend, Kling's relations with his fellow policemen have been good. After losing his initial greenness, he goes through a period during which he gets along well with everybody, especially Carella and Meyer. The crisis of Claire's murder leaves him with a compulsive harshness that causes him to be bawled out by Cotton Hawes for playing the Lord High Executioner during an interrogation and by Steve Carella for his insistence on searching Cindy Forrest for a gun when she comes to the squad room in connection with the death of her father. Things finally get so bad that Byrnes wants him out of the 87th Precinct permanently. His breakup with Augusta is just as traumatic, but by that time Kling has developed a maturity that permits him to control his hostilities: his response to Willis's story about a cheating husband is to leave the room. Apparently his growing maturity is also recognized by Ambrose and Bartholdi, those talented comics at the Missing Persons Bureau, who at last stop making Kling the object of their humor. Finally, Kling displays a wholesome realism in his attitude toward a no-good cop like Andy Parker, insisting that he be invited to the wedding because failure to do so might get him killed some time when he and Parker are partners.

Steve Carella recognizes that one of Bert Kling's strongest assets is a kind of basic decency that civillians can recognize, which causes them to confide in him. Such trust has been won hard by Kling, and it has followed much the same pattern as his improving relations with the other cops. He puts down the snobbish elevator operator in Stewart City and the man who uses the word "nigger" in his presence, but he shows real constructive skill in questioning five-year-old Monica Boone. He develops a sensitivity for people's feelings, recognizing that he has acted like a "goddamn Nazi" in a too-severe questioning. Kling does not hesitate to use force when appropriate. His quickness with a gun saves Carella in *Doll,* and saves himself on two later occasions, but he throws his gun away when he catches Larry Patterson making love to Augusta (*Heat*).

Chiefly, though, the story of Bert Kling is the story of his loves: three big ones with Claire Townsend, Cynthia Forrest, and Augusta Blair, and two minor ones, with Anne Gilroy and Nora Simonov. Another big one (Eileen Burke) may be developing at the end of *Ice.*

Kling as a lover is driven by a fundamental fear of women and a simultaneous need for sex to be unfailingly good. The fear arises out of a sensitivity that makes him dislike questioning women because they are inclined to cry, and they make him uncomfortable when they do. Anne Gilroy scares him, and so does Augusta Blair. The fear is apparently related to an almost obsessive need for sex to be "good": trying to make up his mind to marry Augusta, he very pointedly questions Carella about whether it is "still good" between him and Teddy. The knowledgeable Augusta recognizes this anxiety and relieves Bert of the symptoms during their first real sexual encounter, using a hammer as a therapeutic device.

His need to be in love is compulsive; on the verge of the breakup with Cindy Forrest, he makes himself believe he is already more than half way in love with Nora Simonov, merely because he is seeing her as witness in the case he is working on. Kling of course lacks the cool control of Cotton Hawes, who also enjoys a constant need for women but without Kling's head-over-heels commitment.

Significantly, there is no "type" among Bert's successive loves. Claire Townsend is a serious and committed student who makes Phi Beta Kappa in her junior year at Women's U. and who later becomes a dedicated social worker with a real talent for working with her patients. Cindy Forrest is also professionally oriented, studying for her M.A. and planning to go for a Ph. D. in psychology, but in contrast to Claire's seriousness Cindy is capable of a kind of nuttiness that prompts her to send a six-foot plywood Valentine to Kling in the squad room. Augusta Blair is the most self-sufficient of the three, who takes her modeling seriously and who displays remarkable ability in handling the psychopath who intends to rape and murder her. All three are physically beautiful but in different ways, from Claire's coal-black hair and regular features to Gussie's overwhelming red-headed splendor. The absence of type is even more pointed with Kling's two "minors," as between Anne Gilroy, who comes on like an amorous tornado, and Nora Simonov, who coolly avoids Bert's probes.

What Kling is seeking evidently, is a completely submissive, reliant woman like Teddy Carella or Christine Maxwell, but he has not found her. He was most successful as protector to Claire Townsend, whom he did help to face her emotional hangups, but he was no help to Cindy Forrest, not being around when she was attacked.

Kling changes more than any other character in the series, and the changes are phased by his love-life. From the time of his first appearance until Claire Townsend's death he is the ebullient innocent, energetic, learning, generally making a good impression. His worst period, between *Lady, Lady, I Did It!* and *Eighty Million Eyes,* is characterized by deep depression, a degree of hostility that almost ruins him professionally, and finally the catharsis in his shooting of the woman who is about to kill Carella. The next cycle is a short one, corresponding to his affair with Cindy Forrest, and ending with their breakup in *Sadie When She Died.* This period represents a developing maturity in Kling, both personal and professional; he can take the departmental kidding in stride, and although the sight of the mutilated shotgun victims makes him physically sick, he has no trouble dealing with several dangerous characters during this time. After meeting Augusta Blair in *Let's Hear It for the Deaf Man* he regains some of his old bounce, which stays with him until the disaster in *Heat.* The bitter Kling of *Ice* reminds us a little of the same figure in

Doll, except that Bert now internalizes his pain instead of directing it into outward hostility.

There is one special feature of Kling's successive love-lives that should not escape notice: he meets all five of these women on the job, as victims or possible witnesses in cases he is working on. The same set of circumstances brought together Steve Carella and Teddy, Cotton Hawes and Christine Maxwell, and it is a reminder of the social isolation of police life that makes it almost impossible for cops to establish meaningful relationships outside their small vocational sphere.

Chapter 10

Cotton Hawes

Roger Broome thought the name was "Horse" when the two detectives entered his room on that February afternoon in the process of questioning the tenants of Mrs. Dougherty's rooming house about the theft of a refrigerator. Roger had correctly heard the name of the shorter one, which was Willis, but not that of the tall one, a red-headed policeman with a jagged white streak across his temple. The scene is a heavily ironic one, because Roger has been debating all day whether he should tell the police how he had killed Molly Nolan the night before, and how Molly's body is now in that same refrigerator at the bottom of the river. Nevertheless, the red-haired detective impressed Roger in two ways. First, he was courteous, carefully spelling out his name for Roger, H-A-W-E-S, and generally treating him as a respected adult. Moreover, he was knowledgeable, even familiar with the location of Roger's home town upstate.[1] The paradox is completed four years later when Roger Broome, under the influence of too much alcohol, makes a public confession. Predictably, it is Cotton Hawes who remembers him, even recalling his name from that brief interview.

Cotton Hawes was born in Boston, the son of Jeremiah Hawes, a Protestant minister with so strong an admiration for Cotton Mather that he named his son for him. That name has created some problems for Detective Hawes (though not to the extent that Meyer Meyer has suffered as a result of his father's whimsy), and he has debated changing it, but has apparently reconciled himself to gratitude that Jeremiah Hawes did not feel so strongly about the elder Mather and christen his son Increase.

103

At any rate, Cotton Hawes received from his Boston upbringing two lifelong directions. One is a standard of conduct that leads him to try at least to be a good and decent man like his father. The other is a saturation in the Boston sense of reality that keeps him from straying too far from the truths inherent in a situation, together with an almost puritanical respect for logic.

We do not learn much of the history of Hawes during adolescence, except that he went through a period of believing that the ultimate happiness is to be enjoyed in the sexual relationship and that he stage-managed a production of *Henry V* in high school.

During World War II Hawes served, with a Chief Torpedoman's rating, on a PT boat in the Pacific. The boat had the distinction of delivering a devastating attack on a Japanese dock installation on a tiny island, and Hawes himself the distinction of having once slept through a kamikaze attack.

Before his transfer to the Eight-Seven, Hawes had served in the 30th Precinct, one of those wealthy areas in the City about as different from the 87th as could be imagined. It was during his assignment to the 30th that Hawes received the knife-wound that resulted in the white streak over his temple, in a story that has been re-told almost as often as that of Meyer's name. That white streak has come to produce almost magical effects on different kinds of people, at one time conveying an impression of menace and at another stirring the passions of susceptible women.

Hawes has at his command a greater variety of detective skills than his colleagues, being as intuitive as Carella and even more logical than Meyer. In one of his most impressive triumphs (in *Killer's Payoff*) he plays a hunch that leads to the solution of an old crime which in turn permits him to solve the present murder case. Across the board, though, he is much better at logic than intuition, as in that remarkable feat, in the same story, of tracing Sy Kramer's automobile route by studying his gasoline tickets. Hawes' police skills are distinctly superior: he has a specialist's knowledge of guns, he is an expert at interrogation, and he is cool and brave in a crisis. Hawes is at his best in his handling of Virginia Dodge in

Killer's Wedge, first in his attempt to trick her, and when that plan fails and Teddy Carella is in danger, he faces Virginia down in a contest of raw courage. It is typical of him, though, that even at the height of the crisis he is ashamed of himself for hating Virginia Dodge so deeply, and when he has conquered her he can not deliver the judo chop that would break her neck.

Hawes' outstanding successes have been those in *Killer's Payoff*, in which he is distinctly the star; in *Lady Killer*, where he catches the connection between "the lady" and George Laddona and prevents the murder just in time; and of course in *Killer's Wedge*, when he saves the whole squad from annihilation. *Storm* is completely his show, providing him the opportunity to call upon his command of logical reasoning. He also plays an important part in the solution of the murders in *Like Love*, relying here not on logic or intuition but upon his erotic experience of Christine Maxwell.

Despite his skill, Cotton has been caught off guard and beaten up three times, most humiliatingly in *'Til Death*, where he is creamed by the gorgeous Oona Blake.

On the personal side, Cotton Hawes finds it necessary to cope with an ongoing contest between his innate superiority and his basic sense of decency. When the two qualities are in conflict, or more particularly when the sense of superiority gets out of control, he has a bad time with his colleagues. This is the case when he first transfers into the 87th in *Killer's Choice*; his humorless arrogance makes Brynes and Carella nervous, and Meyer describes him as "a regular whiz," a very dangerous reputation for a policeman or anybody else who works in a comradely organization. Hawes' saving quality is his decency, which shows itself, in different ways, in the fact that he has learned not to equate slum-dwellers with criminals, in his never having shot an animal or caught a fish unless he was hungry, and even in his having trouble remembering to call Lieutenant Byrnes "Pete." It is when his intelligence is governed by this basic decency that we see Hawes at his best. When the news of Steve Carella's death in *Doll* reaches the squad, Meyer is overcome with quiet grief, Kling almost destroys himself with self-reproach, but Hawes goes to a Western movie in an effort to forget, a rational enough act, though not a satisfying one.

As in the case of Bert Kling, Hawes's career can be gauged in terms of the women in his life, with one important difference: Hawes, we are told, can "fall in and out of love with consummate ease," and we may well believe it. Busily engaged in trying to redeem himself from the blunder that almost got Carella killed, he expediently declines the proposition of the lonely woman in the apartment house, but his trip up to Kukabonga Lodge in *Killer's Payoff* is more leisurely, and it is marked by a series of sexual conquests. Hawes is not promiscuous in his love-life, as witnessed by the number of women who have tried unsuccessfully to seduce him, besides the apartment house tenant in *Killer's Choice:* "Lady" Astor in *Lady Killer,* Liz Bellew (presumably) in *King's Ransom,* the stripper in *Give the Boys a Great Big Hand,* Martha Tamid in *Like Love,* and the superintendent's wife in *Bread.*

Hawes meets and falls in love with Christine Maxwell during the investigation in *Lady Killer,* and he maintains a reasonably steady commitment to her thereafter, with one notable defection. This, of course, was his snowy week-end at Rawson Mountain Inn with Blanche Colby in *Storm.* Blanche fades from the story after their return to the City, but Hawes is still dating Christine in *Blood Relatives,* though he has no intention of marrying her.[2] Otherwise, he continues to attract the attention of women and to be attracted by them, though that game has been apparently scoreless.

The relationship between Cotton and Christine has been completely carnal, apparently untroubled by any of those emotional complications that have sometimes upset the love-life of Bert Kling. Hawes holds Christine by means of his prowess as a lover, and she restrains him through a clever incitement of jealousy. The practice of both controls is evident during that day in *'Til Death* when Carella calls Cotton to ask him to be present at his sister's wedding. Christine does not want to go, but Hawes "talks" her into it. At the party after the wedding, Christine goes off into the bushes with one of the guests for a necking session just because she enjoys the excitement.

We must not end this discussion without noting that Hawes has been subjected to a significant reduction of role. Since his big moment in *Storm,* he has not enjoyed any success of the magnitude of the ones in *Killer's Payoff* and *Killer's Wedge*. He still plays an essential part in the work of the squad, as when he saves Carella from the ax murderer or when he recognizes the Zero in one of the Deaf Man's mischievous picture-clues. Otherwise, it seems certain that Hawes has been deliberately eased out of the spotlight to avoid his unduly overshadowing the others.

Chapter 11

The Second String

In the article on the 87th Precinct in *The Great Detectives,* Ed McBain compares his detective squad with a family. Lieutenant Byrnes is, of course, the father. Meyer is the older brother, Carella the next oldest, Kling the youngster, Hawes the cousin who came in from another precinct to become an adopted brother.[1] The family analogy is apt, suggesting the ideas of innate unity and basic ties of loyalty, but it is also a reminder that a continuing series must have a cast of characters in which most of the roles are assigned in order to satisfy certain pre-conceptions: in a police story the audience expects at least a token Black, a Puerto Rican (in the Western U.S. he would be a Mexican), a clown for laughs, a black sheep (on a police squad he might be either a crook or a sadist, or both), and a little guy who will fool you with his strength and prowess. If the writer is short on imagination he will fill up the list with stereotypes who do and say the expected things. If he is a master of fictional creation, like McBain, he will satisfy our expectations and also make those characters genuine people each of whom belongs in the story and is yet an individual in his own right.

When we speak of the second-string people in the series, we refer to those who play roles that carry a share of the narrative somewhat lighter than that of the Regulars, Carella, Meyer, Kling, and Hawes. Most of the people we will disucss in this chapter have been on the scene for quite a while, and they show up in about one story out of two.

Lieutenant Peter Byrnes
Byrnes is there right at the beginning of *Cop Hater,* and we

see more of him in *The Pusher* than in any other story, but it is not until Virginia Dodge is holding the detective squad at bay with a bottle of nitro and waiting for Steve Carella to come in so she can kill him that we begin to get an insight into Pete Byrnes' conception of leadership and his feeling for his squad.

Killer's Wedge has one of those double-meaning titles, referring to the little wooden wedge used in the murder Carella is investigating and the big moral wedge Virginia has driven between Byrnes and his squad. Not just once but twice the Lieutenant is faced with a choice between cold-bloodedly sacrificing a member of his team and sacrificing himself and all the rest of the squad. If the question were a simple one of giving his own life, Byrnes would not hesitate, but the real mark of his sense of leadership is his refusal to act solely on an objective calculation of the odds.

Byrnes's leadership is paternal, mixing a strong demand for authority and discipline with a fatherly concern for the welfare of his people and their families. He chews out Steve Carella more often than anybody else, but the possibility of Carella's death pains him as if Steve were his son. He blasts the squad for lack of progress on the murders in *Ice,* at the same moment that he is passing a box of Valentine candy among them.

Lieutenant Byrnes's case is a good example of the mutual influence in the police procedural between the policeman's job and his family. In *The Pusher* the Byrnes family go through a crisis occasioned by the son Larry's becoming a drug addict and almost having a murder pinned on him. Peter Byrnes handles Larry in the same way he handles the detective squad, lovingly but sternly. He succeeds, but only because of the sacrificial support of Harriet, one of the most admirable people in the series. When the crisis has passed and Byrnes apologizes for neglecting her during the case, Harriet's response is, "Peter, I married a cop."

Arthur Brown

Detective Arthur Brown may present a reader with some perceptual problems, in that he is a black policeman (almost unconscionably, the only black detective in a heavily black precinct) who takes pride in his color and resents slurs on his race, and at the same time does not want to think of himself as a Negro. In this respect he is much like many other minority policemen in fiction (John Ball's Virgil Tibbs is a good example) who want to be judged on the basis of their professional abilities alone, and policewomen like Lillian O'Donnell's Norah Mulcahaney who feel the same way about their sex.

There are three kinds of people whose racial attitudes irritate Arthur Brown. The first is those whites who automatically undertake to be superior to any black person, like the desk clerk at the ratty Hotel Carter who greets him with "We don't take niggers" before he has a chance to state his business and whom he utterly squelches, or the Georgia-born Suzie Endicott, whom he delights in terrifying. The second group is composed of those white phonies who consider it hip to call blacks "spades" and to make jokes about watermelons. Then, there are those black lawbreakers who think all they need to do is to say to him, "Come on, brother, give me a break."

Arthur Brown has achieved a balanced outlook on himself and his profession. He does not, as he tells Geraldine Ferguson in *Jigsaw,* lust after a black Cadillac or a white blonde, and he can joke about his color, as he does in *Fuzz* when he puts on a pair of white gloves for handling evidence, and goes into a minstrel routine for the benefit of Hal Willis.

Brown's most frequent professional assignments are undercover jobs and buggings, both of which he does well. On the streets with an air of youthful innocence in *The Con Man* he skillfully traps the two cheap con artists who try to victimize him with the old pearl switch. He is somewhat less successful in *Jigsaw* where, disguised as a crook named Arthur Stokes he infilitrates a shady operation but finishes the campaign with a cracked head. His first bugging job is the assignment to eavesdrop on the blackmailed Lucy Mencken in *Killer's Payoff,* a task that bores him so severely he reads the *National Geographic* on the job. In *Fuzz* he is assigned to the wiretap on the La Bresca phone because he has a knack of knowing what is important and what is not.

Like most of his fellow detectives, Arthur Brown experiences value conflicts between his natural sympathy for people in trouble and his need for security as a member of the community. Thinking about a child molester who has just been picked up in the precinct, Brown wonders why he must be punished when he really needs help; then he remembers his own seven-year-old daughter, and the world seems suddenly too complex.

The Puerto Ricans

As with the single black policeman on the squad, it may appear odd that there is only one Puerto Rican, and that the second one does not enter the story until the first one is killed. Once again we must remind ourselves that in the well-told story characters are selected for dramatic balance rather than realistic probability.

Frankie Hernandez plays two parts in the 87th Precinct saga. As a member of the squad he serves as liaison between the police and the Puerto Rican community, a capacity both groups find useful. The other detectives come to him for advice and information, and the Puerto Ricans come for protection from the law. This intermediary position makes Hernandez's job much harder, but it also allows him to anticipate and prevent trouble, as when he stops Andy Parker from beating a young Puerto Rican and a little later in the same story when he prevents a street-gang murder.

As a character Frankie Hernandez plays another part, the admirable romantic who stands out in contrast to some of the cruddier ones, especially Andy Parker. Frankie is set up in sharp juxtaposition to Parker twice, first in *Give the Boys a Great Big Hand*, where he refuses to be angry with Parker, even when Parker pushes him to the point where Steve Carella gets into a fight with him. The other is in *See Them Die*, in which Hernandez is killed by the cornered criminal Pepe Miranda: Frankie volunteers to go after Miranda because "a Puerto Rican wins" whichever way things turn out, acting according to a nobility of purpose that accents the animal brutality of Parker, who keeps pumping bullets into the body of Miranda, who has killed Hernandez.

Hernandez is replaced by Alexiandre Delgado, another cop who knows how to deal with Puerto Ricans, but Delgado's methods are authoritarian and pragmatic in contrast to Hernandez's idealism. Delgado has made only one important appearance, investigating the beating of Jose Huerta in *Hail,*

Hail, the Gang's All Here! His handling of that case is a good example of "street justice," the informal system under which a great many troublesome problems are dealt with unofficially. Delgado knows the Puerto Rican community well enough to recognize a conspiracy of silence that can not be broken and also the administration of communal justice that will effectively put an end to Huerta's dope-pushing. Delgado does not pursue the matter.

Hal Willis

Willis is another of those second-string durables who have been around from the beginning. He is the classic example of how deceiving appearances can be: barely tall enough (5'8") to make the police force, Willis is compared at one point to a happy gnome and at another to an alert cocker spaniel, but he is a judo expert who has been known to throw a four-hundred-pound man.

Willis' record as a cop has been quite good. It was he who trapped Gonzo into admitting he had shot Carella, who successfully tailed Lucy Mencken after Meyer had lost her, who successfully questioned Hamling about the Lewis Scott murder when his real target was Hamling's girl friend, and who easily took the dangerous Al Brice when he was wanted for questioning in the investigation of the disappearance of Augusta Kling. His only area of weakness has been in acting as backup for Eileen Burke; twice he has failed her, once when she tried to decoy the mugger and again when she undertook the stake-out of the Dirty Panties Bandit. In neither case was Willis really culpable, having mis-judged an apparently harmless diversion on the first occasion and having been diverted into another case on the second.

Undoubtedly one of Willis' assets as a detective is his control over the informant Fats Donner. Like most other cops who use informants, Willis gives Donner a long leash and overlooks all those infractions for which Fats could be sent up for the rest of his life. He draws the line in *Fuzz*, though, when he finds Fats keeping a fifteen-year-old in his apartment; Willis makes some heavy concessions to force him to give her up.

Considering his remarkable effect on women, it is a wonder that Willis is still single. Because of the Mutt and Jeff phenomenon he has an amazing attraction for the tall ones (once dating a five-niner who was madly in love with him), but he practically also devastates tiny Elaine Hinds, whom he and Brown visit in the course of the investigation of the Tinka Sachs murder. Only Eileen Burke has been able to upset his aplomb, as she did after the great stuck-zipper foul-up on the stakeout in Grover Park in *Fuzz*, but Willis is able to joke about even that when she returns to the precinct for another job years later.

Dick Genero

Detective 3rd/Grade Richard Genero has fired only one pistol shot during his police career, and he has received one gunshot wound. The only thing worth comment here is that they were the same shot. Readers of *Fuzz* will recall the episode, the same one in which Detectives Willis and Burke were trapped in a sleeping bag. In that monumental fiasco Genero did not look much worse than the others, but he has looked worse than anybody else ever since.

The representation of Genero is another good test of the parameters of realism in the police procedural. It may not be too much of a strain to believe that there are cops as dumb as Genero; the real trial of our credulity is our willingness to accept the possibility that he has sense enough to find his way home after work. All questions of reality aside, of course, Genero's role in the story is that of buffoon, and in that capacity he has been good for several chuckles.

In a sense, Genero's level of competence is an intimation of the plight of law enforcement sunk to its lowest level. Consider, for example, the manner in which he supplies the solution to the big question in *Ice*, simply by walking into the squad room with his transistor radio going full blast and thus personifying the unpredictability of the breaks in police work. Consider also the manner in which his ignorance supplies the solution to another and more general problem about men who hate paper work. Unable to spell anything with more than two letters, Genero is never able to cope with "perpetrator" and "surveillance," and so abbreviates them to "perp" and "surv" in his reports, initiating a practice that is soon adopted by others in the squad.

The Roughnecks

Every family, says Ed McBain in the article in *The Great Detectives*, has its ne'er-do-wells (93), and the 87th Precinct series has had three: Roger Haviland (who was killed in *Killer's Choice*), Andy Parker (still one of the regulars) and Ollie Weeks (a member of the 83rd Squad who has worked with the Boys from Grover Avenue on three cases). Actually these three do not have a great deal in common: Haviland was the only certifiable sadist among them, Parker the only slob, Weeks the only literal stinker. The one quality they share is that nobody wants to work with any of them if he can get out of it.

Roger Haviland is on the scene at the beginning, a giant bull of a cop who threatens to break the arm of a young suspect who talks back to him. In *Cop Hater* we learn that he was once a gentle cop who tried to break up a juvenile street fight, suffered multiple fractures for his pains, and after an exceedingly painful recovery (during which his arm would not heal properly, had to be re-broken and re-set) came out of the hospital with a determination to spend the rest of his life evening the score with the criminal world. Haviland loves to slap people around, and his favorite indoor sport is questioning suspects, especially when he is the only cop present.

His death is one of those blatant ironies that characterize the series. Seeing a wounded man sitting on the curb, Haviland elects to do the first decent thing in years, gets shoved through a plate glass window, and dies of a severed jugular. Several things come to light after his death, including the not surprising fact of his participation in a petty graft scheme.

Having killed Haviland, McBain says in the same article, he realized he had made a mistake, because every family *must* have its SOB.[2] Thus he created Andy Parker, who shows many of Haviland's unloveable qualities and who in addition is lazy and incompetent, something Haviland was not. Each of them was transformed into a bully as the result of a street ambush, but it should not be forgotten that Haviland got his beating as a result of an *effort* (breaking up a fight), while Parker got his as a result of *avoiding* action (administering "street justice").

Among other things, Andy Parker is a bigot who considers any member of an ethnic minority fair game for his crude sarcasm. He calls Frankie Hernandez "Chico," refers to the criminal Pepe Miranda as "your brother," then accuses Hernandez of being touchy when he resents the association. His laziness is fabulous,to the extent that the vexatious painters in *Fuzz* almost throw a drop cloth over him while he sleeps at his desk.

Parker comes closer than any of the other cops of the 87th to being an unmitigated scoundrel; he shows no regard for the feeling of the father of the kidnapped boy in *King's Ransom,* he kids a lab man about his wife's "knockers," and when he gets shot, nobody cares. It is a mark of McBain's craftsmanship, though, that he will not leave Parker as a reprobate only. When word comes that Steve Carella has been killed in *Doll,* Parker goes to a prostitute, lets his grief go in the form of verbal abuse, finally buries his head in the pillow and mutters, "He was a good cop."

Ollie Weeks, a detective in the 83rd Precinct up in Diamondback, is really not such a bad creation for those who are willing to overlook his egregious racial bigotry, his physical stink, and his barbaric manners.

Detective Weeks, known also as Fat Ollie, enters the scene in *Bread,* during an investigation that spreads over into Diamondback. He has made two appearances since, and is otherwise hanging just over the horizon and threatening to get a transfer into the 87th, for which he has developed an enormous affection. Carella and the others hope this will never come to pass: Meyer considers him "a vast uncharted garbage dump," and Carella shudders at the prospect of Brown, Meyer and Delgado on the same squad with Ollie, to whom they are "jigs," "kikes" and "spics."It should be noted also that he possesses some limited talents as a comedian, doing a trite imitation of W.C. Fields and a passable one of a German SS officer.

The one big quality that differentiates Ollie Weeks from Haviland and Parker is that he is a capable detective. It is probable that Augusta Kling would not have been rescued without the good work of Ollie, who first suggests the use of wedding photographs to identify the abductor and then gets a make on the vehicle by having a witness examine pictures of a number of different makes of trucks. He has a practical approach to problem-solving that reminds us (if the comparison is not too odious to Hillary Waugh's readers) of Chief Fred Fellows.

Collectively, McBain's second-stringers constitute a good illustration of the workings of formula in popular fiction. Regardless of the dictates of plausibility, or realism, there are certain things the reading public wants in police stories, and the writer who deviates very far from those expectations runs a risk of losing his customers. At the same time, the writer must be sufficiently inventive to inject fresh elements, otherwise the material will not hold our attention. The convention of the sadist on the squad is firmly enough fixed to call for the procession of Haviland, Parker, and Weeks through the stories, but McBain knows better than to make them exact clones of each other. The presence of the squad *schlemiel* has also gained acceptance, to the extent that Richard Genero is quite admissible as the only purely one-dimensional character in the series, without a solitary redeeming quality.

Chapter 12

The Back-Ups

In this chapter we will deal with three kinds of police: those three intermittents who are associated with, but are not members of, the detective squad, Captain Frick and Sergeants Murchison and Miscolo; one detective who has been assigned to the 87th for three special jobs, Eileen Burke; and a member of the detective squad who has made only brief occasional appearances, Bob O'Brien.

One observation should condition the discussion that follows: the 87th Precinct is not only a man's world but a young (or at least middle-aged) man's world.

Eileen Burke

Anybody who has wondered why there is only one black and one Puerto Rican on the 87th Detective Squad should also ponder the question of why there has never been a woman with a permanent assignment. In each of her appearances to date, Detective 2nd/Grade Eileen Burke has been sent over from headquarters for a specific job. The only other policewoman to play a part in the stories was Detective 3rd/Grade Alice Banion, who was hurriedly drafted for the questioning of Margaret Redfield in *Ten Plus One* and has never re-appeared.

Each time Policewoman Burke is introduced into a story, the "woman" side is accented much more heavily than the "police." She is invariably described first in terms of legs (always "sleek and clean, full-calved and tapering to slender ankles"), breasts and hips. This is not to suggest that McBain makes of Eileen Burke a sex-symbol or sex-object. She is a capable police detective, a person of considerable courage and physical independence, though she does tend to be somewhat dependent emotionally. She has a piquant sense of humor that comes through especially in *Fuzz* and *Ice*, in her twitting Willis about what really happened in that sleeping bag in Grover Park.

Eileen's sexuality gets much more intense emphasis in *Ice*, than formerly. First, there is the rape-fantasy she confides to Bert Kling, in which a rapist she is trying to arrest succeeds in his purpose with her and "turns out to be Prince Charming," with whom she falls madly in love. Then, at the end of the story, when she has succeeded in the arrest of a rapist (who turns out to be not Prince Charming but a fourteen-year-old boy), she appears at Kling's door with the request that he make love to her.

Actually, Eileen is following a pattern established earlier in the series (and indeed not unfamiliar to all readers, movie-goers, and TV-watchers of the latter twentieth century) of regarding sex as the solution to predicaments and the celebration of involvements. It is most evident in the relationships of the Carellas: when Steve and Teddy face a crisis, when Teddy becomes upset, when they are celebrating a success, they make love. Teddy's one besetting fear is of the time when Steve will no longer be attracted to her. It is obvious too in the scene in which Carella calls to ask Cotton Hawes to be present at his sister's wedding, when Hawes is spending the week-end with Christine Maxwell: Cotton averts a crisis by taking Christine back to bed, after which they arise and go to the wedding. The fetish of sex-as-fulfillment is pervasive in the story of Bert Kling, who is obsessed by dread of the time when love-making will no longer be good. It seems only natural, then, that Eileen, after a shattering experience, should seek release by spending the night with the man whose own commitment to the ideal of unfailingly good sex has been frustrated.

The Oldsters

The three policemen in the 87th Precinct who have occasional minor roles—Frick, Miscolo, and Murchison—are uniformed cops, not detectives. They are all older men, who share the quality of inflexibility and inability to adapt to new circumstances.

Captain John Marshall Frick is officially in command of

the whole precinct force, including the detective squad, but he has at least the good judgment to leave that operation to Peter Byrnes, who knows how to handle it. Which is just as well, because Frick is less than helpful in every case in which he becomes involved. He fails to see the point of Byrnes's weird telephone remarks during the Virginia Dodge crisis, and when Augusta Kling is abducted his fuddy-duddy ramblings delay the planning until Carella purposely interrupts him. As a rule Captain Frick is portrayed as the incompetent administrator who spends his office hours fiddling with time-sheets and such, and he rarely appears to advantage.[1]

Sergeant Alf Miscolo operates the clerical office of the 87th Squad, and it is typical of McBain's handling of his minor people that he gives Miscolo not only a tag but a history.

The tag is Miscolo's fussiness in running the clerical office, which he does with the "clearheaded mercilessness of an Arab stablekeeper," resenting interruptions like the demands on him for first aid ("Next time go to a hospital") and coffee ("What is this, Howard Johnson's?"). The history develops when Miscolo is shot by Virginia Dodge and in his delirium calls for "Mary": his wife's name is Katherine. Mary, we are told at this point, was part of Miscolo's pre-World War II experience in the Navy, where he was too old to serve when war actually came.

Like Frick and Murchison, Alf is getting on in years. We learn in *Ice* that he is retiring in three years, but the standard symptoms of advanced age are already evident at the time of the first visit of the Deaf Man, when Miscolo wants to talk to Carella about two things but can't remember what the second one was.

Great events in the 87th squadroom are frequently presaged by a phone call, "This is Dave at the desk downstairs," the caller being of course Desk Sergeant Dave Murchison, a stout man who does not like to climb stairs. As is the case with most of the other people associated with the precinct, Murchison's best and worst sides come to light during the Virginia Dodge affair: he races up to the squad room when he hears the shot fired (the one that almost kills Miscolo), but he fails to see the significance of Byrnes's pointed use of the word "forthwith" during their brief conversation and consequently misses the chance to get help.

There are not many "messages" in the 87th Precinct series (or anywhere else in mystery fiction, for that matter), but one that comes through with special force is the affirmation of the current nightmare regarding old age. We see it clearly in the anxieties of Bert Kling and Teddy Carella, both of whom are obsessed by the dread of loss of sexuality, which translates into the horror of becoming turnips like Frick, Miscolo, and Murchison.

Bob O'Brien

O'Brien is the only member of the 87th Squad about whom a legend has grown up. Unfortunately for O'Brien the legend is uncomplimentary, and more unfortunately still, it has strong support in fact. Most of his fellow policeman shy away from answering a complaint with Bob, because, regardless of the nature of the squeal, there is almost certain to be some shooting, none of it O'Brien's fault. There is another side to him, though, in the fact that he has the best record in the City for finding missing teen-agers.

Of all the members of the 87th Squad who have been around since the early stories, McBain has used O'Brien the least, with the exception of the shadowy DiMaeo, who usually shows up only as a name on the roster or as a voice in a general squadroom conversation. It may be that the O'Brien legend is too costly to sustain very often, as Meyer finds out in *Ghosts* when the two go out on a call and Meyer ends up in the hospital with two bullet wounds.

The first Oriental cop in the series, who could become a back-up or a second-stringer, shows up late in *Ghosts,* making his entry as a young patrolman, like Bert Kling and Richard Genero before him. Takashi Fujiwara, whose decisive action leads to the arrest of the perpetrator in the Craig murder, is a member of the detective squad in *Ice,* on friendly terms with Carella and apparently accepted by the others.

Chapter 13

The Stand-Bys

Our survey of the people of the 87th Precinct saga concludes with a look at three individuals and small groups who are not part of the precinct police force and who make periodic but fairly important appearances: the Deaf Man, the several pairs from Homicide, and the informers. In this category we can place Sam Grossman, head of the police lab, whose role we discussed in Chapter 4.

The Deaf Man

He has shown up three times, at unpredictable intervals of eight and five years. His intellectual brilliance and his powerful personal appeal place him in the Master Criminal class. The Deaf Man could be the Professor Moriarity of the Eight-Seven except for a weakness that inevitably makes him overplay his hand and almost insure his own defeat. If he should ever settle down to business and quit fooling around with the cutesy stuff, the Deaf Man could conceivably paralyze the whole process of law enforcement in the City.

His appearance in *The Heckler* is almost a materialization of the Father of Evil. His first murder shatters the Eden-like calm of Grover Park; he is a diabolically handsome fiend whose sexual wizardry reduces a nineteen-year-old waitress to a state of imbecility; finally, he bombs and burns large areas of the City without regard to unnecessary loss of life and property, but this magnificent caper is ruined by the innocence of a lone hungry patrolman at the Isola terminus of the Majesta ferry.

Apparently, this episode is all that is needed to prod him into an obsessive drive to punish the cops of the 87th Precinct for spoiling his show. When he returns in *Fuzz* he compels himself to change his plans for a series of murders of city officials in order to commit one inside the Precinct just for the satisfaction of showing up the stupidity of the Eight-Seven Squad, and in so doing runs into a piece of fantastic bad luck that not only foils his scheme but gets him wounded by the gun of Steve Carella. So, in *Let's Hear It for the Deaf Man,* he expends as much energy propounding riddles to the police as he does in planning the bank robbery and—once again—is so scrupulous in playing the game that he tips his hand to Carella, who again ruins the climax for him.

With each of his appearances, the Deaf Man has become less lethal. The toll in *The Heckler* includes one man cold-bloodedly killed so "L. Sordo" can assume his identity, plus a number of casualties from bombing and arson almost too great to count. In *Fuzz* he again guns down two city officials to enforce his extortion plan, but his climactic attempt comes apart in John Vincenzo's tailor shop. In *Let's Hear It for the Deaf Man,* the only knot he raises is on Steve Carella's head, and the only three people killed are the Deaf Man's own accomplices. He also becomes less villainous. In *The Heckler* the emphasis is on his power of cold calculation and his capacity for almost truly scientific precision. In *Fuzz,* this power degenerates into a machine-like logic and an increased emphasis on making the police look foolish. Finally, in the big plan for holding up the First Federal Bank on Van Buren Circle, the planning with reference to the police becomes eccentric and cranky instead of coldly logical.

The abatement of villainy is evident too in his diminished role as dominant male. His sensual artifice, which renders the little waitress completely helpless in *The Heckler,* is replaced in *Fuzz* by a crude sadism that forces a pitiful female junkie to strip and dance in return for a fix. Later in the same story the Deaf Man has taken on a young mistress, whom he treats kindly and even patronizingly in spite of her stupidity. He dominates her sexually, but with none of the macho intimidation he practiced on the waitress. In *Let's Hear It for the Deaf Man* he has no woman except for the two who are on his hit teams, and his dealings with them are strictly workaday.

Stephen Knight argues that the Deaf Man novels belittle the threat of professional crime, and he compares them to the crime-comedies of Donald Westlake.[1] It might be closer to the mark to consider the successive tonings-down of the Deaf Man's menace as another evidence of McBain's special transformation of reality. The Deaf Man's exit-line in *The Heckler,* as he swims underwater when his first bank caper fails, is pure menace: "Well—next time." At the end of *Fuzz* a cosmic transmutation seems to be in the making, as Genero watches the bloodstained trail lead away to "perhaps the rest of the world," but his departure from *Let's Hear It for the Deaf Man* is straight expediency: seeing Carella arrive at the bank and knowing the jig is up, he quickly gets the hell out of there.

Homicide

When Alexander Pike, the photographer at Bert Kling's wedding, first hears them mentioned, he thinks Monoghan and Monroe must be an old vaudeville team. In any other context the misunderstanding would be absurd, but to the reader of the 87th Precinct stories those two (or Carpenter and Calhoun or Forbes and Phelps) may seem more like an old-style comedy pair than the traditional homicide inspector at a murder scene.

Regardless of the tags they may be wearing in a given story, they are essentially the same pair, with their alliterative names, their antiphonal speech, and their Tweedledum-Tweedledee look-alike demeanor. They are almost inevitably lazy, complaining about being called out at inconvenient hours and, unless contrary evidence is overwhelming, suggesting suicide as a quick solution. They are insensitive, making coarse jokes at the murder scene, and authoritarian. It is hinted at least once that they are more susceptible to graft than the average: how else could Monoghan and Monroe have "nice places down in Miami"?

One notable exception to this pattern is also a significant clue to the nature of the police sub-culture. This is the occasion when Carpenter and Calhoun come out to the precinct house to question Kling about his shooting of Carella's woman captor in *Doll.* They are vastly more considerate than usual, and although they make a couple of feeble tries at inappropriate humor, they want to get their routine task over with as little pain as possible to Bert Kling, a reminder of the adage that policemen always stick together.

Evidently McBain felt his way into the unique treatment of his homicide cops. The un-named pair that are on the scene in *Cop Hater* before the arrival of Carella are more like the city cops we expect in the realistic police story, hard-bitten and sarcastic. It is not until Monoghan and Monroe come after Patrolman Kling in *The Mugger* that we begin to see some glimmer of future development; they echo each other's remarks, and although they are more grim than in later appearances, they are already beginning to show some talent for banter. By the time of *Killer's Choice* they are in high gear, the antiphonal effect having assumed such dominance that Carella even chimes in at one point, prompting Monoghan to remark, "Everybody wants to get in the act."

"The act" proved so successful a stylistic device that McBain extended it beyond the practice of the boys from Homicide. In *Blood Relatives* Monoghan shows up alone (Monroe has 'flu'); so what happens? Within one page the medical examiner comes in on the refrain, and the act goes on as expected. Notice, too, how when the Homicide pair are not around, the performance is often furnished by others, like the pawn shop owners in *Lady Killer,* the boys of the Missing Persons Bureau in *The Con Man,* the painters in *Fuzz,* and the garbage men in *Blood Relatives.*

The Informers

We have discussed the informers used by the 87th Squad as components of police method and as part of the police sub-culture. Now we must take one more look at them, as series characters; they are, McBain says, members of the police family, like "distant uncles on the outer fringes."[2]

Usually the stool-pigeons in police fiction are nondescript bums who snitch for the price of a bottle of cheap wine, but not those of the Eight-Seven, each of whom is a pro in his own way. Danny Gimp is not a criminal but a natural-born gossip. Fats Donner is a drone with expensive tastes. Francisco Palacios operates a quasi-legitimate business.

Danny Gimp's real name is Nelson; the name by which

everybody calls him is the result of a limp occasioned by a childhood bout with polio. Danny's whole life is a bitter commentary on the inverted values of society. He has a gift for collecting information, sorting and evaluating it, and he might have become a brain in the world of finance except that he was born on Culver Avenue and has consequently been forced into devoting his talent to the absorption and transmission of gossip. Danny served a prison term for a crime he did not commit, thus acquiring the credentials demanded by the underworld for access to its secrets.

The real quality of Danny's character lies in his fidelity to Steve Carella, whom he considers his friend. He never asks more than a standard payment from Carella for his services, and when he hears Steve is dying (in *The Pusher*) he foregoes the offer of money from Byrnes in exchange for a chance to visit the hospital room. Like most other informers, Danny works exclusively for one cop, though he has been called upon by others.

Fats Donner is another matter entirely. Fats knows no loyalties except those to his mountainous self, and he will work for any cop who approaches him, provided the price is right. It is Willis who keeps Donner on the leash, having enough on him to send him up for twenty years but holding off as long as Fats co-operates.

Thus Fats Donner walks that thin line between satisfactory production as an informer and value as a potential collar. Again in contrast to Danny Gimp he is an essentially nasty person whose ideals of the good life run to young girls, Turkish baths, and winters in Vegas and Miami, all purchased with shady means. At the same time, he is a good source of information and can usually deliver on schedule.

Fats is characterized by a kind of tacky polish that punctuates his speech with expressions uncommon in the world of crime, like *comme ci, comme ca,* and *entre nous.* Most readers should be thankful for his speedy recovery from the beat-talk that characterized his first appearance (in *The Mugger),* full of things like "Clifford. The name's from nowhere. Hit me again."

The third recruit to the ranks of the informers, Francisco Palacios, did not come onto the scene until recently, and he is

McBain's first ethnic informer. Palacios operates in the El Fierno neighborhood of Diamondback a store specializing in occult materials, which is really a front for a porn shop. He is much more businesslike than either Gimp or Donner, dealing with the cops as one professional to another.

In contrast to his homicide men, who are so much of a pattern that people can't tell them apart, McBain sharply differentiates his informers, giving them unmistakable identities.

Chapter 14

The Telling of the Tales

Consumers of popular crime fiction can be conveniently grouped into three classes. The first consists of those readers—by far the majority—who swallow the stories wholesale, obtaining satisfaction from suspense and sensation, and likely to be uncritical as long as the narrative does not stray too far from the accepted norms. A second and smaller group would be made up of those readers who bring to crime fiction some fixed preconceptions, including finely tuned social and moral consciences and some literary standards based upon the traditional consensus. A third group—the smallest by far—is composed of those who find in the stories an opportunity for interpretation that can tell us something about the nature of popular culture.

The first and third of these should experience no problems with the 87th Precinct series. The second group evidently does so, particularly if their standards of police-story writing are grounded in the novels of Ngaio Marsh or even those of Joseph Wambaugh. To this group evidently belonged "Newgate Callendar," the *New York Times Book Review* critic who on one occasion expressed wonder at the popularity of the McBain books because "he turns them out by formula" and who consigned the McBain style to "the rough-hewn-features-and-flinty-blue-eyes department.'[1] Here also we can find those readers who are annoyed by the occasionally playful mood of many of the accounts or by the fact that in the stories pure detection sometimes leads nowhere in the solution of those crimes that are solved by sheer luck.

It is especially important at the beginning of a discussion of the literary qualities of the 87th Precinct series to remind ourselves of the almost unique special tone of the accounts, because otherwise they are easy to mis-read. What should be the reader's attitude toward a tale of criminal investigation shared by Monoghan and Monroe and the other assorted clowns from Homicide? With what degree of seriousness do we take a series in which the author "emerges" in a sequence of photos on the dust jackets? McBain's identity as Evan Hunter was known early in the development of the saga, but he coyly appears in those pictures once in a crowd of thousands, once as a member of a shadowy trio, later in Ivy League attire reflected in a sylvan pool, later still peering demurely through an ornamental screen, and at last (on *Long Time No See*) in full suede-jacketed array as himself. Just to put matters into perspective, the reader might try to imagine a similar "emergence" by John Creasey from the pseudonymous J. J. Marric or Elizabeth Linington from Dell Shannon.

This is not of course intended to suggest any unseemly frivolity in the 87th Precinct stories but to remind ourselves that irony and paradox pervade the series from that description of the sparkling illusory City as a stage set on the first page of *Cop Hater* right on through the appearance of Miss Bailey and the "cockroach-men" in the same story, reminding us that "the protecting wall of play," as Northrop Frye aptly calls it, is always there.[2]

The ironic tone is most obvious in those fantastic situations that have become a trademark of the series, like the Great Stakeout in *Fuzz*, where all carefully planned police strategies fail, but the suspect halts when simply ordered to do so, and where two criminal groups foil each other's plans, inadvertently doing the work of the police, who are foolishly helpless. The comic element is strong, as it is in Roger Broome's confession to an airtight-perfect crime in *Shotgun*. Sometimes, though, we get the surprise without the humor, as at the end of *Heat,* when Bert Kling does not even recognize the man who has made two attempts to kill him. Occasionally the irony is brutal, as in the case of the parolee in *Ten Plus One* who is trying to go straight, is framed by the police and sent back to Castleview, or the burglar in *Sadie When She Died,* who commits suicide just as he is being exonerated of murder.

The ironic flavor makes itself felt in almost every other

aspect of the series. It is clear enough in those switches of theme, where the anti-Semitic motive fails to develop in *"J"*, where it is almost assured, but comes through in *Lady, Lady, I Did It!*, where it is quite unexpected. Several of the titles have an ironic twist, like *He Who Hesitates,* where the story is a direct denial of the proverb. Then, of course, there is the irony of personality, that gets Roger Haviland killed while he is doing the first compassionate thing he has undertaken in years. McBain seems to underscore the irony of Haviland's death by giving his successor Andy Parker exactly the same motive for his own brutality, but without any hint of Haviland's one concession to decency.

Much of this, if told with a perfectly straight face, would be ludicrous, but on the slanted screen of the illusory City and the warped calendar it seems quite in place.

Any assessment of the overall tone of the 87th Precinct saga must recognize that the comic spirit permeates the series to a greater degree than may be found in any other police mysteries. McBain makes strong use of comedy for the conventional purposes of relief, always as a coolant to keep the narrative atmosphere from becoming too muggy. The pattern is set in *Killer's Choice:* first, a gruesome description of the murder in the liquor store, relieved at once by the appearance of Monoghan and Monroe; a few pages later the cycle is repeated, first with the outpouring of bitterness by the victim's mother, mitigated immediately by Bert Kling's conversation with the ingenuous Monica. The refusal to let anything harsh stand for very long substantially becomes the policy of the series, showing up in *Ice* in that scene where Lieutenant Byrnes bawls out the squad for lack of results, then passes around a box of Valentine candy with an admonition about squeezing chocolates and then not eating them.

The reader accustomed to the candid spirit of the series will not be surprised at McBain's occasional comments on the narrative art, as when he tells us how the scene he is describing would look projected on a screen. Ed McBain has a fine gift of burlesque, and it is a rare 87th Precinct story that does not contain some sharp parody of a literary absurdity, like the one on avant-garde poetry in *Shotgun,* in the memorial verses read by Margaret Ryder's beat friends; or the sample of publisher's hype in *The Con Man,* a blurb on "The Tattered Piccolo" as the greatest novel since *Gone With the Wind;* or that catalogue of the formulas and stereotypes in popular fiction developed in conversation between Bert Kling and Eileen Burke in *Ice.* Comments on narrative method, one's own or other people's, would seem completely alien in any other crime series; in the ironic scene of the 87th they are quite normal.

For a writer whose style has matured as markedly as McBain's has, it is surprising to observe how little his bag of narrative tricks has changed during the writing of the 87th Precinct stories. The pattern is fairly well established in *Cop Hater:* the double-barreled title, the atmospheric use of weather, the facsimile reproduction of police forms, the nut-witness, the detailed accounts of police methods (especially lab techniques), and the lyric narrator. All of these devices, plus some others that came into the series later, have been the stock in trade of McBain the storyteller.

We might comment on at least one device that emerged after *Cop Hater* and has become another McBain trademark, the use of visuals as essentials in the narrative. There are the little pictures representing Teddy's hands spelling out "I love you" in sign-language in *Lady, Lady, I Did It!,* the samples of handwriting in *Ax* and *Hail, Hail, the Gang's All Here!,* the ads featuring Tinka Sachs in *Doll,* the succession of pieces of the puzzle in *Jigsaw,* and the series of photos mailed by the Deaf Man in *Let's Hear It for the Deaf Man.* Quite often these visuals are important clues to the solution of the mystery, but more often they lend plausibility to the account, as little fragments from phone directories, airline schedules, and typescripts.

We need not dwell on McBain's methods for the portrayal of his main characters. Like most of the series people in mystery fiction, they do not change much with the passage of time. Here, though, as in almost everything else, McBain has avoided a standardized pattern; as we noted in Chapters 7-10, Steve Carella tends to go through cycles of moodiness, while Meyer's emotions hold at a fairly constant level; Bert Kling's personal makeup has undergone some marked changes, but Cotton Hawes is substantially the same man he was years ago. The method, as it affects the series characters, is photographic rather than developmental. McBain tends to tag his main people with little qualities that just barely catch a reader's attention. Have you ever noticed, for example, how often Meyer Meyer is catching cold?

With his minor characters, though, the technique becomes much more obvious, and it is not hard to see why even those hundreds of people who make two- or three-page appearances come so close to being unforgettable. The reason is that Ed McBain could not settle for letting anybody in a story, no matter how minor his role, be simply a name and an identity. Everybody has some special dimension. Sam Kaplowitz, proprietor of the photo-engraving shop Hawes visits in *Killer's Choice,* is a good example. The only function of Kaplowitz is to furnish some information, but he must also have his private tag. Whenever Hawes addresses him as "Mr. Kaplowitz" he is corrected: it's *Sam.* So it is with all of them, most markedly with that procession of nuts and oddballs who periodically show up as witnesses and suspects, but also with every elevator operator, taxi driver, and clerk.

Plot, however, is a subject of greater interest to the mystery addict than is characterization or atmosphere. We will spend some time on the construction of the 87th Precinct stories, partly because McBain is especially good at it and partly because his approaches to plotting have been rather broadly misunderstood.

The normal structure of a police procedural novel is a number of separate story-strands, unrelated to each other except by the coincidence of being simultaneously under investigation by the same police teams. Sometimes the commentators on McBain's work write as if this is the only kind of structure he uses. Stephen Knight does not go so far, but he does give pre-eminence to the multiple plot:

> ...The essential structure of a McBain novel is not fully formed until the fourth novel *The Con Man,* though strong aspects of it are present in the earlier books. This presents more than one narrative line, and different police investigate several cases simultaneously. A multiple, even a fragmented structure and a plurality of heroes is created. This is most fully seen in later novels like *Fuzz* and *Hail, Hail, the Gang's All Here....*[3]

If by "essential structure" we mean *typical* structure, then we are talking about the single narrative line, often involving more than one investigation plus spinoffs and complications, but still one plot. *Fuzz* and *Hail, Hail, the Gang's All Here!*, far from being typical, were unique in structure until the appearance of *Ice.*

I think we can best approach the subject of structure with a quick overview of the types of plots encountered in the 87th Precinct series:

I. Single Plot (*Cop Hater, Lady Killer, Calypso,* etc.)
Usually, all the action is directed toward a single problem. There may be minor distractions, like the cruddy couple in *Give the Boys a Great Big Hand,* or the story may involve a considerable number of related cases, as in *Cop Hater* and *Calypso.*

II. A. Two Major Plots Related by Subject (*The Pusher*)
The single example to date is *The Pusher.* The subject of both the Hernandez plot and the Larry Byrnes plot is drugs. Note that the Byrnes plot is not a spinoff, because it develops early and gets as much attention as the other.

II. B. Two Major Plots Related By Theme (*Killer's Wedge, Heat*)
In *Killer's Wedge* the "wedge" is actual in one plot, symbolic in the other. The same may be said of the heat in the Newman murder and in Augusta Kling's illicit affair.

III. A. Major-Minor Plots Related by Subject *(The Con Man, Like Love)*
The Con Man is the pure example. The big con is practiced on the women in the major plot, the little one by the pair in the minor plot. In *Like Love* the relationship is suicide.

III. B. Major-Minor Plots Related By Coincidence (*Killer's Choice, See Them Die, Eighty Million Eyes, Fuzz, Hail, Hail, the Gang's All Here!, Ice*)
Eighty Million Eyes is the classic example. The only relationship between the Gifford murder and the Cacciatore assaults is that they are under investigation at the same time.

IV. Major (Plus Minor) Plot Plus Spinoff (s) (*Killer's Payoff, Lady, Lady, I Did It!, The Empty Hours, Ax, Ten Plus One,*

Sadie When She Died, Long Time No See, Ghosts)

The spinoff develops as an outgrowth of complications in a major plot and is given independent treatment. For example, the story of the rape and manslaughter of Eileen Glennon in *Lady, Lady, I Did It!* grows out of the investigation of the bookstore massacre, though it is not part of the original problem. The principle applies in cases where the outcome of the present case is dependent on the solution of an old one: *Killer's Payoff, The Empty Hours, Ten Plus One, Long Time No See, Ghosts.* The Corey murder in *Ax* is triggered by the ax murder, though not part of the original problem. The Simonov story in *Sadie When She Died* is like that of Eileen Glennon: hidden under the original problem, it comes to light as a result of the first investigation. Note that this pattern is the closest McBain comes to the residual mystery technique of the tradition of Raymond Chandler and his successors.

V. (Variation On I.) Apparent Single Plot Becomes Two Actual (*The Mugger, 'Til Death)*

In *The Mugger,* the death of Jeanne Paige seems to be part of the Clifford plot and is treated as such until the resolution. The same for the several attempts on Tommy Giardino in *'Til Death,* which appear to be the work of the same person(s) until the end.

As long as we are making lists, let's catalogue some of the more obvious conclusions from these patterns:

1. The norm is the *single plot,* which is the pattern of almost half the stories to this point. Thus, McBain does not follow the parallel plot characteristic of the police procedural, as J.J. Marric (John Creasey) does in the Gideon stories.

2. The most complex story to this point is *Hail, Hail, the Gang's All Here!*, which with its multiple plotting is so different that it stands alone.

3. The time-frame of an 87th Precinct story tends to be slightly more than one week. (See Appendix E). Fewer than half the stories span a week or less. The longest to date is *Ten Plus One* (six weeks), necessary because of the large number of individual cases,

which could hardly be accomplished in less time.

4. There is no obvious correspondence between time-frame and complexity of structure. Note the variation among the one-day stories: *Lady Killer* (single plot), *Killer's Wedge* (two major), *See Them Die* (major-minor), *Hail, Hail, the Gang's All Here!* (multiple-parallel), and so on. The same is true of those with a time span of a month or longer.

5. The structure tends to run in cycles. After the complicated plotting of *Let's Hear It for the Deaf Man* we have a series of tight one-plot no-spinoff stories (*Hail to the Chief* through *So Long As You Both Shall Live*), then after a minor spinoff in *Long Time No See,* one more single-plotter (*Calypso*) before returning to the major-minor pattern in *Ghosts.* The tendency is to follow a single-plotter with one or more of the same, then back to complications for a stretch.

In connection with Type IV. (Major Plot With Spinoffs) we should note one for the People-Who-Live-in-Glass-Houses Department. The reader may recall Steve Carella's somewhat caustic remarks in *Long Time No See* (109-10) about "California mystery writers" with a penchant for old crimes that go unsolved for years until some contemporary sleuth digs them out and solves them. Carella may have forgotten for the moment how many 87th Precinct cases could not be solved until he and his colleagues dug back into some past infractions, like the ones in *Killer's Payoff, The Empty Hours,* and *Ten Plus One*—or, for that matter, the one he was working on when he made those unkind observations, which was at least partially dependent on the solution of a murder committed during the VietnamWar.

Ed McBain is one of the most inventive of writers, but he has repeated certain situations at least once, such as the woman victim with a multiple personality (*Killer's Choice, Sadie When She Died, Doll*); the child witness to murder *(Doll, Hail to the Chief)*; the killer who wants to be caught (*Lady Killer, Calypso*); and the mistreated wife who will not complain against her husband (*"J"*, *Like Love, Hail, Hail, the Gang's All Here!, Blood Relatives*).

We must not leave a discussion of McBain's narrative craftsmanship without at least commenting on his use of weather in the creation of atmosphere. All the way from the stifling heat of *Cop Hater* through the numbing cold of *Ice,* the reader must be aware that weather plays a more important role in these stories than in most procedural accounts. Generally, the weather serves four kinds of purposes in the 87th Precinct stories. It may be used only as a backdrop, to keep us reminded of the time of year, as in *Lady Killer.* It may serve to reflect and re-inforce the feelings of the people in the story, like the unseasonable October chill in *King's Ransom.* It sometimes accents the basic idea of the story, like the heat in *Cop Hater* that intensifies the sexual tensions between Hank and Alice Bush. On occasion the weather is indigenous in the mystery itself, like the blizzard in *Storm* or the rain in *Give the Boys a Great Big Hand.* McBain has never undertaken to make weather a thematic symbol (like the fog in Ross Macdonald's *The Chill*), though he does come close in *Ice.*

The 87th Precinct stories are crime stories, but they are also mysteries, and we can not make an adequate assessment of their literary qualities without an overview of the novels as instances of the mystery tradition and, more specifically, as examples of the police procedural type of mysteries.

It hardly needs saying that Ed McBain does not write mysteries in the Golden Age tradition of Agatha Christie, but like any other detective story writer he uses many of the techniques of the formal-problem or pure-puzzle type of narrative. We can gain some notion of McBain's special handling of these tools by looking at the way he uses two of the standbys of the mystery craft, clues and deduction.

Especially in the earlier books, McBain demonstrated that he could tuck in a clue with as much finesse as could Dorothy Sayers. While the police are puzzling over the identity of "the Lady" in *Lady Killer,* there appears a character named Laddona. The police do not see the connection; neither in most cases does the reader, but if we later turn back to see whether our author has played fair, it is clear that the solution was right there all along. He uses the same type of linguistic clue in *Lady, Lady, I Did It!*, when the question is about Joseph Wechsler's use of the word "carpenter"; Mrs. Wechsler refers to the "car painter" on the same page (90). In the later books, employment of the formal clue becomes less obvious, but the substitute is even more effective. In *Let's Hear It for the Deaf Man,* for example, the Deaf Man unloads an avalanche of pictorial clues on the Boys from Grover Avenue. Over the phone he twits Carella about the picture of the Zero, pointedly using the word "circle" in several different senses. This time, though, the hint is not allowed to stand; Carella gets it on the next page (191).

Another basic of the mystery is the process of deduction, which varies all the way from the "ratiocination" (as Poe called it) of the intellectual genius of the classic novel to the canny, practical-minded processes of the private eye of the hard-boiled tradition. The 87th Precinct detectives can do it either way: in *Doll* there is a nine-step exercise in deduction that Ellery Queen would not be ashamed of; in *Lady, Lady, I Did It!* Steve Carella works out an analysis of the observations of the four wintesses that is a model of empirical logic. As a rule, though, the cops do their deductive thinking on the run, or in unstructured brainstorming and snowballing sessions

There are a number of traditional detective story devices sprinkled through the series. There are the dying clue in *"J"* and the time-honored gambit of the series of murders to conceal the real motive (*Cop Hater, Long Time No See*). We recognize another old standby, the murderer who assumes the identity of his victim, in *The Heckler, The Empty Hours,* and *Shotgun,* and the phony newspaper story planted by the cops (*Eighty Million Eyes*), the same one Poe's Dupin used to flush out the owner of the orang-outan in "The Murders in the Rue Morgue."

Some of the more obvious tricks, like the red herring, are missing, but the split-second timing used by the murderer in *Killer's Choice* is strongly reminiscent of the high-jinks played with railway time-tables in the old stories. Moreover, the cops occasionally resort to the Big Bluff (e.g. *Bread,* 162 ff.) in the best style of Nero Wolfe and others.

Some of the earlier stories manifestly place too-heavy demands upon the reader's credulity, as when five-year-old

Monica Boone in *Killer's Choice* is able to repeat verbatim a three-page telephone conversation with the killer. In two of the stories the reliance on coincidence is dubious: once in *'Til Death*, when two would-be murderers, completely unknown to each other, go after Tommy Giardino on the same day; again in *Fuzz*, where two criminal groups hit an obscure tailor shop for entirely different reasons at the same moment. This kind of inexpedience, though, disappears from the later novels, along with some other stylistic rough edges we will discuss a little later.

More to the point, though, is the classification of the 87th Precinct stories in that type of mystery known as the police procedural. McBain's series is generally considered to be the near-perfect example of the procedural story, partly because he has been more successful than most other writers in making his detection a real team effort, and partly because his handling of police methodology is unsurpassed. Besides these qualities, though, the 87th Precinct series has gone further than most in development of the myths of the procedural and in commitment to the procedural formula.

One of the basic myths of the procedural class is the conception of law enforcement as the war between Good and Evil, and its antithesis, which holds that there are no absolutes of black and white in the struggle but only intermediate shades of gray. The 87th Squad are divided in their allegiance to the two viewpoints: Steve Carella sees law enforcement as simply the good guys against the bad guys, and Arthur Brown agrees. Meyer Meyer, on the other hand, is not always sure which are which. Another myth, this one unanimously accepted, is the perception of police work as the war that can never be won, the battle that must always be fought over.[4] We usually sense the persistence of this one at the end of a story like *Ten Plus One*, where a long, difficult investigation has been completed, but almost before the men of the Eight-Seven have a chance to re-hash it the telephone rings: "Here we go," says Kling.

We must take special note of the procedural myth of the Unsolved Case,[5] because McBain has been willing to develop it more fully than any other mystery writer. This is a tradition adopted from real life, where it is definitely *not* myth (far more cases are unsolved than are solved), but in police fiction is talked about more than it is practiced. The most extreme example in the 87th Precinct series is the murder in Chapter 14 of *Like Love*: the victim is never identified and the murderer never caught. Needless to say, this is not the main plot of the novel (readers would not stand for an unsolved major mystery), but the police do spend considerable time on it. The Huerta beating in *Hail, Hail, the Gang's All Here!* goes down as officially unsolved, though the reader is left in no doubt as to the perpetrators. Then, of course, there are two murders in *Ice* (Judite Quadrato and Timothy Moore) that are never solved by the cops, though the reader knows who committed each of them. McBain's willingness to make the unsolved case a fictional reality is one evidence of his courage as a mystery writer, and it also adds considerably to the sense of plausibility.

As I pointed out in *The Police Procedural*, the procedural formula can be broken down into five components: 1) The Ordinary Mortals: in contrast to the brilliant eccentrics of the puzzle-type story and the virile private eyes of the hard-boiled mystery, the police in the procedural stories are usually people of a few special endowments beyond their professional competence. 2) The Thankless Profession: police are consistently underpaid and overworked, and are scorned by most of the rest of society. 3) The Tight Enclave: policemen have such strong group loyalties that they protect each other's incompetence and dishonesty. 4) The Fickle Breaks: police detection is quite often dependent upon pure luck. 5) The Tyranny of Time: the longer a homicide investigation goes on, the slimmer are the chances that it will be successful. In the 87th Precinct stories, almost all of these components can be seen at two levels, the verbal and the actual.

Such is especially the case with the convention of the Ordinary Mortals. At the verbal level, it expresses itself as whimsy, as when one of the cops is mortified over a foolish failure and decides to become a fireman or an elevator operator. As a rule, the deprecation is directed at one's own inadequacy, not that of the System. At the actual level, this component is clearest in the incompetence of a slob like Andy Parker or a moron like Richard Genero. Significantly, the social impact of this convention in the McBain series is not as strong as in the novels of Maj Sjowall and Per Wahloo: Genero is really too bad to be true and hence does not represent the social criticism implicit in the representations of the several police klutzes in the Sjowall-Wahloo stories.

Feeling about the Thankless Profession is usually expressed in some such gripe as "Why the hell would anyone ever choose police work as a profession?" At the level of performance, it is most dramatically felt in the sense of imminent danger that hangs over the stories from the shooting of the first policeman in *Cop Hater*, but it also comes through in such matters as the failure of the detectives to be reimbursed for automobile mileage, toll charges and the like.

The sense of the police world as a Tight Enclave pervades the stories. There is no doubt how the others feel about a sadist like Haviland or a bum like Parker, but when Haviland is killed and again when Parker is shot, the force is galvinized into action with an intensity that is not relaxed until the perpetrators are caught.

The accent on the other two is almost completely verbal. Everybody talks about the importance of the breaks, but even the serious bad breaks are customarily met with stoic resignation. The same is true of the time-pressures: in *Ghosts*, Steve Carella remembers the business about the first twenty-four hours of an investigation being the most important, but, significantly, he thinks of the admonition as a "song and dance."

McBain's techniques for developing and maintaining suspense are not original, but they can be remarkably effective. One of the most suspenseful passages in the series is the one in Chapters 17-19 of *The Con Man*: Teddy Carella has spotted Donaldson and his intended victim and undertakes to tail them, while Charlie Chen, who is also aware of the crisis, tries to get word to Steve. The point of view switches from Teddy to the squad-room to Carella at home and back again with the sense of impending danger building until it would be an apathetic reader indeed who could put the book down before the big climax. Somewhat less dramatic but just as effective is McBain's ability to attract our curiosity by introduction of an unknown menace, as at the beginning of Chapter 2 of *Heat*: a strange, sinister man enters the scene without preparation, and he moves with such determination that we know he is bound upon some ominous errand, but we must follow him for several pages to discover that this is Jack Halloran, who is out to kill Bert Kling.

The McBain style is not as distinctive or as easy to recognize as is that of Nicolas Freeling. It is often described as "crisp," but it can be poetic. As a rule, it does not call attention to itself but fits the mood of the narrative. If we want to see how it has matured during the writing of the 87th Precinct series, we need only look back to that conversation between Steve Carella and Miss Bailey in *Cop Hater*: as he listens to her theory about the cockroach-men, we read how "Carella suppressed a smile" and a couple of lines later "Carella answered, amused" (123). This kind of ingenuous stress has never been out of place in the popular crime story, but it has given way in the later McBain novels to a prose that can imply a great deal without having to say everything.

Another evidence of maturing style is the disappearance of the equivocal transition, one of the tricks of style in the earlier books. At the end of a passage of dialogue in *The Pusher* (96) Gonzo tells a companion he is going to call Lieutenant Byrnes "as soon as I check my pigeons." "Check the pigeons!" Byrnes is shouting at the beginning of the next paragraph, meaning of course the informers. The trick is repeated so often that it becomes a trademark, like this one in *See Them Die*:

"Do you know what goes on under the skin of the buildings?" (25)

*   *   *

The skin of the building which housed the uniformed cops of the 87th Precinct .... (26)

It is clever enough, but so obvious that it soon wears out, to be replaced by the longer-range thematic devices like the one in *Calypso* where the description of Castleview State Penitentiary (71) is echoed in the one of the house in the Iodine Islands where Santo Chadderton is a prisoner (159).

Ed McBain's real skill with language is most obvious in his love of the sounds of speech and his fondness for word-play. Consider, for example, how many of the titles of the books have double meanings: the two meanings of "wedge" in *Killer's Wedge*, of "King" in *King's Ransom*, "see" in *Long Time No See*, "ghosts" in *Ghosts*, and at least a half-dozen others,[6] reaching something like world-record proportions when "ice" has four different meanings in that story. The word-games take on something of a recreational quality in those rhythmic exchanges involving Monoghan and Monroe, the painters in *Fuzz*, the garbage men in *Blood Relatives*, and others. Then, of course, there are most obviously those lyric flights in praise of the City that seem never to wear out.

The dialogue in the series has consistently attracted favorable attention. Critics and reviewers seldom fail to comment on the sharpness, the deadpan comedy, and the special ability of McBain to build whole chapters around passages of dialogue, to the extent that few writers would dare to venture. On the whole, the passages of dialogue that are most successful as narrative are those that carry the story along without apparent strain, though we are occasionally treated to a piece of showcase humor, most notably when Eileen Burke, returning to the scene in *Ice*, says to Willis, "You were hoping for Raquel Welch, maybe?" an allusion designed to elicit a chortle from those readers who recall the cast of the movie *Fuzz*.

McBain largely stays away from formal symbolization, to the extent that its appearance in *Ghosts* is almost startling. Steve Carella, spending the night at a motel in Massachusetts with Hillary Scott, faces one of those close encounters with illicit sex and this time barely escapes. In his bathroom the next morning he sees "a long black hair curled like a question mark against the white tile of the sink" (168), an overt signal to the reader of the nature of Carella's problem.

There is a passage in *Calypso* (39-45) in which the artistry with words, the love of antiphonal echoes, and the skill in dialogue come together to produce a markedly dramatic effect. This is the passage in which Carella is reading the calypso lyrics from George Chadderton's notebook at the same moment a black prostitute is being murdered. As the scene switches between the squadroom and the dark street, the lines of the song form a commentary upon the plight of the woman caught in a mesh from which there is no release except in her death.

McBain has done one other unusual thing in the 87th Precinct series, in supplying a stylistic strand that runs from story to story and tends to cement the whole together. This is the use of a kind of preparation, usually below the level of the reader's consciousness, that paves the way for big developments. We get an early sample of the device in *King's Ransom*, in a brief mention of (among other odds and ends down at the police lab) a bloody human hand wrapped in a newspaper, and of course that hand figuratively comes to the fore in the next story as the major image in the subject and the title.

There is another early preparation in *Ax*, when Steve Carella tells a seven-year-old there is no such thing as ghosts, an assertion he comes to doubt later. A broader and more fundamental instance is the preparation for Bert Kling's refusal to kill Gussie and her lover when he catches them at the end of *Heat*. We get one anticipation of the development as early as *Shotgun*, when Bert asks Carella if he would kill Teddy if he found her with some man. No, Steve answers. Preparation for the basic problem is made in *Let's Hear It for the Deaf Man* when Kling, watching Augusta pose, wonders how many personalities she has, and how many he will get to know. None of these signals catches the reader's conscious attention at the time, but each adds to the groundwork for developments that seem to be natural and predictable outgrowths of the earlier foreshadowings. Such delicacy is not really essential to a mystery series, and its very presence is testimony to a high order of craftsmanship.

Chapter 15

The Eight-Seven Is Not the World

There are a number of mystery writers whose stories seem to invite interpretations beyond the normal boundaries of the tale of suspense. Frequently the applications are implied in the social criticism in the stories, notably in the novels of the Swedish husband-wife team, Maj Sjowall and Per Wahloo, and in those of the American John D. MacDonald. Sometimes, though, the story will suggest a more nearly universal application, as with Raymond Chandler, Ross Macdonald and Robert Parker, whose work hints at archetypal and even cosmic interpretations.

Not so with the 87th Precinct series of Ed McBain: whatever else the Eight-Seven may be, it is no microcosm. It may at first seem open to such interpretation, with its melting-pot mixture of ethnic groups and its range of socio-economic levels from dismal poverty to blatant affluence, not to mention the broad sample of humanity represented in the hundreds of people who have crossed its pages. There are even passages that seem to be leading into a projection of the Precinct as the whole of society and the condition of twentieth century man, but they never develop. What we have instead is a tightly self-contained world in which the topology of space is such that the boundaries of the Precinct can slide back and forth to accommodate the necessities of the story, and time can move at different rates, so that two events that happened on the same day long ago have now become separated from each other by years.

Most especially, the series is light on social criticism. McBain purposely declines full development of the plight of his ethnic minorities, allowing Meyer to take an objective view of his inheritance, Brown to refuse to think of himself as a Negro and the Puerto Rican cops to leave the scene completely. As for the women in the stories, they seem satisfied to fill roles that are supportive of their men: Teddy Carella and Christine Maxwell as sexual delights, and Sarah Meyer and Harriet Byrnes as domestic mainstays. Remember, too, that there have been no policewomen on the Squad since 1962: Eileen Burke is still an outsider. Significantly, the one full-fledged attempt at social-political criticism, *Hail to the Chief*, is one of the weakest stories in the series.

The same holds true for any attempt to represent universal values. To find just one gesture in the direction of allegory we must go all the way back to *The Heckler*, where the first incursion of the Deaf Man into the City is narrated in a sequence of events that look very much like the images of Tranquility shattered by the introduction of Evil, followed by Chaos and Apocalypse, until Evil is defeated by Innocence. McBain can do this kind of thing very well, but he has never repeated the performance in the 87th Precinct saga.

Many critics have seen an analogy between the searches of the lone private investigators, notably Chandler's Marlowe, Macdonald's Archer and Parker's Spenser, and the quest of the Grail by the knights-errant of medieval legend.[1] The only member of the 87th Squad with any kind of noble quest was Frankie Hernandez, whose personal Cause was the dream of the day when Puerto Ricans could be accepted as good guys, but that dream perished in the shoot-out with Pepe Miranda in *See Them Die*, and the idealistic Hernandez was replaced by the pragmatic Delgado, who has no illusions about the psyche of his people.

Nor do the rest of the Boys from Grover Avenue have any with regard to the work they are paid to do. As usual, it is Steve Carella who bespeaks the consensus of the squad, the precinct and the series. On that occasion when Meyer undertakes to twit him about the nature of detection, which is faith in the fictional triad of Motive, Means and Opportunity: "Everybody knows that," says Meyer. "Except me," Carella replies. "I just do my job."

Appendix A

Bread, Random House, 1974
Blood Relatives, Random House, 1975
So Long As You Both Shall Live, Random House, 1976
Long Time No See, Random House, 1977
Calypso, Viking, 1979
Ghosts, Viking, 1980
Heat, Viking, 1981
Ice, Arbor House, 1983

Appendix B

The City: Some Special Problems

1. How large is the 87th Precinct?

The first time the Precinct is described in *Cop Hater* (and a number of times later) we are told that the Eight-Seven is thirty-five blocks long (10), but its width is never stated except for something like "a short [stretch] from north to south," from the River Highway (or, in one story, Silvermine Road) to Grover Avenue. Counting only those avenues that are named, we get a width of six blocks: River Highway to Silvermine Road, to the Stem, to Ainsley, to Culver, to Mason, to Grover. If the transverse is made outside the span of Mason, the width is only five blocks.

In at least two stories, though, we have indication of a considerably greater width. In *He Who Hesitates* Roger Broome tries to remember the location of the bar where he had met Molly Nolan, and recalls walking "six or seven blocks ... straight south on Twelfth Street" from Mrs. Dougherty's rooming house, located at Twelfth off Culver (61). Such a walk would be patently impossible in a precinct as narrow as the one assumed, because Roger would, after a couple of blocks, find himself in Grover Park. Now, it may be argued that Roger was so badly confused that he did not know how far he had walked or in what direction, but there would remain the problem of the employment agency in *Fuzz*, "on the corner of Ainsley Avenue and Clinton Street, five blocks north of the entrance to [Grover Park's] Clinton Street footpath" (37). Here again, counting only the familiar avenues, we can account for three blocks, but not five.

One explanation is that there are a number of avenues other than the familiar ones running east and west through the precinct, some of them only a few blocks long, like Mason. This solution would account for some of that large number of avenues (Crichton, Independence, Base) that are named casually only once and never located.

2. Where is the waiting room of the Isola-Majesta ferry?

That waiting room is where the Deaf Man and Rafe study the ferry schedule and where the Deaf Man makes sure there will be room for his truck to get over to Majesta at the time of the big caper (*The Heckler*, 86). Later we learn that this waiting room is located on the *River Harb* (242), on the opposite side of the island from Majesta, from which point the ferry would have to circle half the island on each trip. This could be considered a simple confusion of rivers, as happens elsewhere, except that the author makes such a point of its location on the Harb, well away from the big fire in progress on the River Dix.

3. How large is Grover Park?

In *The Mugger* (27) we are told that Grover Park hems in the 87th on the south, but there is no clue as to whether it runs the entire length of the precinct. Here and there we gain some further hints regarding its size, learning that it contains a zoo (*The Pusher*), a statue of Daniel Webster (*The Heckler*), one of General Pershing (*So Long As You Both Shall Live*), and one of General Ronald King (*Ice*), all of which would suggest an area the size of Central Park in Manhattan. Such a dimension seems to be confirmed in *Ice* (74), where the police drive "fifty-odd blocks" from the station house to an address on Grover Park West. Bearing in mind that the station house is located near Seventh, and that the park extends to the east at least to Forty-Eighth, where there is a crosstown entrance (*King's Ransom*, 226), we can account for an east-west length of some ninety blocks for Grover Park.

4. Is Grover Park outside the 87th Precinct?

We are told repeatedly that Grover Park lies within two precincts, the 88th and the 89th, but in *Ax* we find that Grover Park Lake is "well within the 87th Precinct territory" (101), and in *Like Love* (187 ff.) Steve Carella and Cotton Hawes are hard at work on a murder inside the Park territory. There may be at least a partial answer in the statement in *Killer's Wedge* that the precinct territory extends into the Park "on a basis of professional courtesy" (16), but this concession does not really explain the location of the lake.

5. Where is Avenue L?

Avenues with letter names begin to show up in *Hail to the Chief* and *Bread*. The sites of Avenue J, address of the building superintendent's lustful wife in *Bread*, and Avenue Y in the Quarter present no problems, because they are never specifically located. Avenue L does raise some questions, though, because of Roger Grimm's warehouse "on Clinton Street and Avenue L, adjacent to the waterfront docks on the River Harb" (*Bread*, 30). Where does this put Avenue L in relation to the River Highway, which runs the length of Isola along the River Harb? It is possible that Avenue L is a new elevated highway along the river front, or it may be that this is another of those arbitrary name changes that seem to be so common in the City.

Appendix C

A Reader's Guide to Other Precincts

Appendix D

The Precinct Station House

The best way to familiarize ourselves with police headquarters in the 87th Precinct is to take a walking tour of the premises, making special note of those features that have figured in the stories.

As we stand on Grover Avenue looking up at the building, we are likely to be attracted by three things. First, there is no question where we are, because of the two green globes that straddle the doorway, each with the numerals "87" painted on it. Second, we must not miss the fact that the wings of the building, right and left, abut toward the street by a few feet, so that if we look up at the second floor on our right, we will see windows of Lieutenant Byrnes' corner office, which also has windows looking out on Grover Avenue. The third feature of this building we can not miss is its uniformly dingy dirty gray exterior.

We climb the seven gray stone steps from the sidewalk and pass through the heavy wooden doors, whereupon we find ourselves facing the pair of glass doors where Patricia Lowery left her bloody palm-prints on that rainy night in September 1975 (*Blood Relatives*). Through these doors we enter the cavernous muster room and face a high desk that looks a little like a judge's desk; behind it is perched Sergeant Dave Murchison, and on its front a sign gives a stern warning, ALL VISITORS MUST STOP AT THE DESK. Beyond the desk and opposite it is a smaller sign that announces DETECTIVE DIVISION, shaped into a hand pointing up the stairs on our right.

After climbing sixteen metal steps we find ourselves on a five-by-five-foot landing which is dimly lighted by a small grilled window. We should notice, by the way, that all the windows in the station house are covered by a metal grillwork, in deference to the fun-loving youngsters of the neighborhood, who enjoy using those windows for target practice. Now the metal stairs double back upon themselves, and we must climb another sixteen risers before we reach the second floor.

We will pause momentarily at the top of this flight to take note of two frosted doors on our right, marked LOCKERS. Immediately on our left is a wall switch that works the lights in the squad room; this was the switch that Arthur Brown unfortunately flipped just as Cotton Hawes had gone to so much trouble to plunge the squad room into darkness in an effort to separate Virginia Dodge from her gun and that bottle of nitro in *Killer's Wedge*. Before moving from our position at the top of the stairs, though, we want to take a look at the door we are facing across the corridor, labeled simply INTERROGATION.

Turning left down the corridor, we pass first, on our right, what was originally intended as an elevator shaft but is now an alcove occupied by a bench without a back, and on our left another wooden bench, this one slatted. Proceeding down the corridor, just before reaching the detective squad room, we find ourselves flanked on the right by a door labeled MEN'S LAVATORY and on the left by one marked CLERICAL, inside which we may catch a glimpse of Alf Miscolo working on his files or maybe brewing some of what is reputed to be the world's worst coffee.

Passing through the gate of the slatted rail divider at the end of the corridor, we are, at last, inside the detective squad room of the Eight-Seven. On our right is a short stretch of wall on which we find the switch that works the six hanging light globes in the squad room, and next to that a bulletin board, a water cooler and a coat rack. Just beyond this stretch of wall is the office of Lieutenant Byrnes, which has been set into one corner of the squad room, so that it has cross-ventilation, with windows looking out on Grover Park and also down at the front steps of the station house. Beyond Byrnes' office, on the front side of the building, are the south windows of the squad room, near which several members of the squad were eating their lunches that day when they became aware that somebody was watching them through binoculars from the park across the street (*Lady Killer*).

Turning now to our left, we can not see much, because two enormous filing cabinets block the view. If we take a few steps inside we can see the part of the squad room that extends to the rear of the building, but we are rewarded by nothing more than a few desks and telephones, and in the far corner the holding cage, where customers of the detective squad are kept until they can be booked.

Appendix E

An 87th Precinct Chronology
July 23-August 19, 1956

The murders of three police detectives during a four-day period lead the members of the 87th Squad on a hunt for a cop-killer, and the bad judgment of newspaperman Cliff Savage nearly results in the death of Steve Carella's fiancee, Teddy Franklin. Patrolman Bert Kling is wounded with a zip-gun. Steve Carella and Teddy Franklin are married.

(*Cop Hater*)

September 12-25, 1956

The City is plagued by a series of thirty-four attacks on women, including one on Policewoman Eileen Burke, by a mugger who identifies himself as "Clifford." The murder of Jeanne Paige is unofficially investigated by Patrolman Bert Kling, who makes the acquaintance of Claire Townsend.

(*The Mugger*)

December 18-25, 1956

The police investigate the apparent suicide of Anibal Hernandez and the murders of Maria Hernandez and Delores Faured, while Lieutenant Byrnes attempts to deal with a case of drug addiction in his own family. Steve Carella is shot and almost killed.

(*The Pusher*)

April 1957

The police are puzzled by the discoveries of the bodies of two women murder-victims, each with a tiny tattoo on her hand. Detective Arthur Brown breaks up the racket of two small-time con experts.

(The Con Man)

June 7 to August, 1957

Annie Boone is murdered in the liquor store where she works. The 87th Squad loses Roger Haviland, who is killed, but gains Cotton Hawes, who transfers from the 30th Precinct.

(Killer's Choice)

June 26-July 17, 1957

Seymour Kramer is gunned down in the best manner of a 1930s gangster movie. The police are successful in dealing with a blackmailer, but Cotton Hawes is singularly unsuccessful in dealing with an assailant on a city street.

(Killer's Payoff)

July 24, 1957

The police are warned that somebody plans to kill "The Lady." Cotton Hawes meets Christine Maxwell.

(Lady Killer)

One Friday Afternoon in October, 1957

Steve Carella investigates a classic locked-room murder. Meanwhile, back at the precinct house, Virginia Dodge holds most of the 87th Squad captive. The Carellas discover that they are about to become parents.

(Killer's Wedge)

June 22, 1958

The wedding of Steve Carella's sister is distinguished by one murder, three attempted murders, and one assault on a policeman. The day's events reach a climax with the birth of the Carella twins.

('Til Death)

One day in October, 1958
A meticulously planned kidnap plot results in the abduction of the wrong boy from the King estate in fashionable Smoke Rise.

(King's Ransom)

March 4-14, 1959
Some especially grisly clues come to the attention of the police, who are investigating the disappearances of a stripper and a musician.

(Give the Boys a Great Big Hand)

April 1-May 21, 1959
The Deaf Man makes his first incursion into the 87th Precinct, commits several murders, and inflicts immense property damage, but is thwarted in an attempted bank robbery. Steve Carella is severely wounded by a shotgun.

(The Heckler)

Sunday in July, 1959
The loyalties of the Puerto Rican neighborhood are divided as the criminal Pepe Miranda holes up for a shoot-out with the police, and Detective Frankie Hernandez is killed in line of duty.

(See Them Die)

August 4-20, 1960
The police, investigating the murder of Claudia Davis, find that she was not who she seemed to be.

(The Empty Hours)

October 13 to November, 1960
Bert Kling's fiancee Claire Townsend is one of four people gunned down in a bookstore. A botched abortion results in the death of a young rape victim.

(Lady, Lady, I Did It!)

Winter (Month and year uncertain)
Cotton Hawes, spending a snowy weekend at Rawson Mountain Inn, helps the local police solve two murders.

(Storm)

April 1-4, 1961
Circumstances surrounding the murder of a rabbi suggest an anti-semitic motive. Meyer Meyer experiences an identity crisis.

("*J*")

Mid-April-Mid-May, 1961
Steve Carella fails to prevent the suicide of a young woman. The police suspect that the apparent joint suicide of Tommy Barlow and Irene Thayer may be a homicide.

(*Like Love*)

April 25-May 31, 1962
A series of sniper killings sends the police back to the investigation of a crime committed twenty-two years earlier. Bert Kling meets Cynthia Forrest, daughter of one of the sniper's victims.

(*Ten Plus One*)

January 3-17, 1964
An 86-year-old building superintendent is murdered in the basement of an apartment building, and four days later a uniformed policeman is killed in that same location.

(*Ax*)

February 12-13, 1964
Roger Broome, in the City on business, gets away with murder because the police are not aware of any trouble except a missing refrigerator.

(*He Who Hesitates*)

April 9-19, 1965
Five-year-old Anna Sachs overhears the murder of her mother. Steve Carella is kidnapped and is feared to be dead.

(*Doll*)

October 13-19, 1965
Comedian Stan Gifford drops dead during his weekly television show. Cynthia Forrest is brutally beaten, and Bert Kling goes after her attacker.

(*Eighty Million Eyes*)

March 4-15, 1968

The Deaf Man returns to plague the 87th Precinct with a monstrous extortion plot. Steve Carella barely escapes being seriously burned by two juvenile sadists. An armed robbery of John the Tailor's shop is foiled, no thanks to the police.

(*Fuzz*)

October 25-November 5, 1968

The police investigate the messy shotgun murders of a couple and the apparently unrelated murder of an off-beat woman poet. Roger Broome drinks too much and gets a troublesome matter off his chest. Bert Kling finds himself caught in a scrap between Cynthia Forrest and Anne Gilroy.

(*Shotgun*)

Early June 1970

The detectives of the 87th Squad try to piece together (literally) a pattern that involves a double homicide committed during a robbery, plus the murders of an habitual criminal and an art gallery operator.

(*Jigsaw*)

One Sunday in October, 1971

During a typical twenty-four-hour period, the police investigate three individual homicides, one multiple homicide, a church bombing, two missing person complaints, two beatings, one poltergeist, one child molester, one juvenile vandal, and a debatable case of lewd and disorderly conduct. Detective Andy Parker is wounded during an armed robbery.

(*Hail, Hail, the Gang's All Here!*)

December 13-25, 1971

Sarah Fletcher is stabbed to death, apparently during the process of a burglary. Bert Kling survives two fights but loses Cynthia Forrest to a psychiatrist.

(*Sadie When She Died*)

April 15-30, 1973

As if the detectives of the Eight-Seven do not have enough on their hands with a kitten burglar and a crucifixion murder, the Deaf Man makes his third encroachment upon the precinct, apparently determined not only to outwit the police but to make them look like cretins in the process. Bert Kling makes the acquaintance of the beautiful Augusta Blair.

(Let's Hear It for the Deaf Man)

January 6-14, 1974

Warfare between street gangs and gangland-style executions spread death and violence into the 87th Precinct. The police come into contact with Randall M. Nesbit, who reminds them of somebody.

(Hail to the Chief)

August 14-17, 1974

Importer Roger Grimm becomes involved in some shady operations that result in murder, assault, and arson. The detectives of the 87th Squad have their first experience with Detective Ollie Weeks of the 83rd Precinct.

(Bread)

September 6-12, 1975

Muriel Stark is stabbed to death on a rainy September night, and the investigation of her murder leads into some of the dark recesses of human abnormality.

(Blood Relatives)

November 9-12, 1975

Augusta Blair marries Bert Kling but disappears on their wedding night. Detective Ollie Weeks enters the investigation without being invited, but his help proves invaluable.

(So Long As You Both Shall Live)

November 18-23, 1976

Three blind beggars are killed in a series of apparently related but motiveless murders. The search for the perpetrator takes Steve Carella into some tragic recent history.

(Long Time No See)

September 15-24, 1978

The murders of two musicians and a prostitute lead the police on a search for a missing person, which ends in the discovery of a bizarre set of circumstances on a lonely island.

(Calypso)

December 21-31, 1978

A writer and his neighbor are murdered, and a few days later an editor dies in an apparently related incident. Steve Carella makes the acquaintance of a medium and goes into Massachusetts to investigate a haunted house. Meyer Meyer is wounded while apprehending a burglar on Christmas Day.

(*Ghosts*)

August 8-15, 1980

Jeremiah Newman is found dead in his mysteriously overheated apartment. Bert Kling escapes two attempts on his life but makes a shattering discovery at home.

(*Heat*)

February 13-20, 1982

The police are puzzled by the fact that three murders, apparently unrelated, are committed with the same weapon. Detective Eileen Burke returns to the 87th Precinct to trap a holdup man and a rapist.

(*Ice*)

Appendix F

Some Crime Statistics

1. Kinds of Crimes in the 87th Precinct Stories

	Primary	Incidental
Murder	56.3 %	19.2 %
Assault, attempted murder	21.7	26.9
Theft, attempted theft *	8.2	31.6
Kidnapping, abduction	2.5	
Drug dealing and possession	2.5	5.8
Arson	1.9	
Rape, attempted rape	1.9	3.8
Mugging **	1.2	
Blackmail	0.6	
Vandalism		3.8
Child molestation		1.9
Prostitution		1.9
Gun permit violation		1.9

* Counting only three cases in *Let's Hear It for the Deaf Man* ("Kitten Burglar")
** Counting only two cases in *The Mugger*

2. Motives for Murder (Primary Cases)

Cover up another crime	22.6 %
Revenge	12.5
In perpetration of another crime	11.2
Self-protection (preventing robbery, blackmail, loss of income; self-defense)	10.1
Financial gain (including extortion)	7.6
Free oneself of a troublesome person	7.5
Insanity *	7.5
Escape detection or arrest	5.0
Jealousy	3.8
Others	11.4
Unknown (unsolved case)	1.3

*The proportion is based on numbers of incidents rather than numbers of perpetrators. Consequently, I have not counted here a murder committed by an insane person with rational motives, like the killing of the locksmith in *Calypso*.

3. Murder weapons (Primary cases)

Pistol	28.2 %
Knife or razor	19.4
Hands, feet, fists	13.7
Rifle	9.4
Drugs, poison	5.7
Blunt instrument	5.0

158

Bomb	2.9
Shotgun	2.1
Fire	1.4
Other	4.3
No weapon	7.2

4. "And a time to die" (Murder by the month, primary cases)

January	8.0 %
February	5.3
March	2.6
April	16.0
May	8.0
June	10.7
July	5.3
August	5.3
September	8.0
October	17.3
November	4.0
December	9.3

Appendix G

Police Injuries in Line of Duty

Name	Date	Hospital	Nature of Injury
Kling, B.	7-25-56	———	shot: shoulder
Burke, E.	9-21-56	(None; first aid only)	beating: face, ribs
Carella, S.	12-22-56	Isola General	shot: chest (critical)
Hawes, C.	7-11-57	(Not hospitalized)	blow below belt
Miscolo, A.	10-1-57	———	shot: back
Hawes, C.	10-1-57	(Not hospitalized)	blows to cheek
Meyer, M.	10-1-57	———	blows to head and wrists
Hawes, C.	6-22-58	(Not hospitalized)	blows to head and face
Carella, S.	4-28-59	Rhodes Clinic	shotgun wound: shoulder; blow to head
Meyer, M.	10-16-60	(None; first aid only)	blows to head
Carella, S.	4-12-61	(None; first aid only)	blows to head and shoulder
Carella, S.	4-18-61	(None; first aid only)	blows to head and neck
Carella, S.	4-12-65	———	blows to face; involuntary **heroin injections**
Fairchild, R.	10-13-65	Buena Vista	blows to stomach, jaw, groin, head
Carella, S.	3-5-68	———	burns on hands
Carella, S.	3-7-68	Buena Vista	blows to throat, head, groin
Genero, R.	3-9-68	Buena Vista	shot: foot; powder burns: thigh

Carella, S.	11-2-68	(Not hospitalized)	blows to head
Carella, S.	11-5-68	(Not hospitalized)	blow to jaw
Brown, A.	6-?-70	St. Catherine's	blow to head
Parker, A.	10-?-71	Buena Vista	shot: shoulder and leg
Kling, B.	12-20-71	————	blows to face, abdomen, chest
Kling, B.	12-24-71	(Not hospitalized)	blows to wrist and throat
Carella, S.	1-29-73	(Not hospitalized)	blows to head and the face
Meyer, M.	12-25-78	Mercy General	shot: leg

Appendix H

Necrology

Policeman Killed in Line of Duty (and
  otherwise)

Detective Mike Reardon   July 23, 1956
  Shot with .45 automatic, twice in
  back of head

Detective David Foster   July 25, 1956
  Shot with .45 automatic, four times
  in chest

Detective Hank Bush   July 26, 1956
  Shot with .45 automatic, chest and
  head

Detective Roger Haviland   June 13, 1957
  Pushed through plate glass window,
  severed jugular

Detective Frankie Hernandez   July, 1959
  Shot twice in chest

Sergeant Ralph Corey, Uniformed
  Branch   January 7, 1961
    Struck on head with wrench

Notes

Chapter 1

[1] *Multiplying Villainies: Selected Mystery Criticism, 1942-1968,* (A Bouchercon Book, 1973), pp. 59, 61.

[2] Introduction to Ed McBain, *The 87th Precinct* (New York: Simon and Schuster, 1959), p. vi.

[3] Ed McBain, "The 87th Precinct," in *The Great Detectives,* ed. Otto Penzler (New York: Little, Brown, 1978), p. 91.

Chapter 2

[1] See Appendix B, Section 1.

[2] Appendix B, Section 4.

[3] So we are told in *The Heckler* (110), but the honor of the highest crime rate was later taken over by the 77th Precinct (*Long Time No See,* 166).

[4] There are sixteen detectives in the 87th Precinct in *Cop Hater* (10) and still only sixteen in *So Long As You Both Shall Live* (11).

[5] Somewhere in this vicinity is Avenue L. See Appendix B, Section 5.

[6] The name first appears as "Grover's Park" in *Cop Hater* (10), but assumes its present form in *The Pusher* (25).

[7] Appendix B, Section 3.

[8] Appendix C.

[9] Newfield is the town where the murder weapon was purchased in *Shotgun;* the Greentree Highway is the route Hawes followed in *Killer's Payoff;* Turman is where Madge McNally was held prisoner in *Hail to the Chief;* Baylorsville is on the route to Fort Kirby in *Long Time No See.*

[10] There is a clue to the speech patterns of the entire region in *He Who Hesitates,* where Roger Broome, from Carey, "upstate," mistakes the name of Hawes for "Horse." This is a mis-perception that would be understandable in the northeastern United States, but it would never occur in the middle west, where "Hawes" and "Horse" sound sharply different.

[11] The general appears in *Like Love* (148). McBain tells the story of the later Herbert Alexander in "The 87th Precinct," in *The Great Detectives,* pp. 90-1.

[12] *The Writer,* 82, No. 4 (April 1969), 11.

Chapter 3

[1] Presented at the annual convention of the Popular Culture Association, Pittsburgh, April 26, 1979. Copy supplied by the author.

[2]One curious enigma in *Killer's Wedge* does not fit any dating scheme. Early in the story (27) Virginia Dodge speaks of the last time she was in the station house, presumably on the occasion of her husband's arrest and trial, "five years, three months, and seventeen days" ago. Assuming the date of *Killer's Wedge* as October 4, 1957, Virginia's visit would have taken place in mid-June 1952. We find out later, however (147), that Frank Dodge's holdup of the gas station (for which he was sentenced and which led to his death in prison) took place in September 1953. Even assuming 1958 as the date of *Killer's Wedge,* this still places Virginia's earlier visit to the station house in June, three months too early.

[3]There are several good reasons for placing *The Empty Hours* before *Lady, Lady, I Did It!* in time-order, the best being the behavior (in *The Empty Hours*) of Bert Kling, who is not suffering the torment he experiences after Claire's murder. In *The Empty Hours* he falls peacefully asleep during a lineup, something he would not have done after Friday, October 13 (66).

[4]I have dated *Lady, Lady, I Did It!* in October 1960 (in spite of the calendar inconsistency) on the basis of the statement (98) that the Carella twins were "almost two and a half years old." Of course the age of those twins gets out of line with the calendar later, but it has not done so at this early date. Even if it had, assuming 1961 as the date for *Lady, Lady, I Did It!* would make the twins *three* and a half, whereas the later inconsistencies always make them *younger* than their calendar age.

[5]Valentine's Day fell on a Friday in 1964, on a Sunday in 1965. When Roger Broome, mailing the money order to his mother, asks "Will that get there tomorrow?" and the clerk answers, "Supposed to," they are obviously not talking about a Sunday (40).

[6]The arrest record of Bernard Goldenthal (143) shows that he was sentenced to 60 days on November 25, 1970.

[7]In spite of the calendar, the events in *Let's Hear It for the Deaf Man* could not take place in 1971, because Bert Kling, who had broken with Cynthia Forrest in December 1971 *(Sadie When She Died)*, takes up with Augusta Blair in this story. References in *Hail to the Chief* (which must be dated January 1974) mandate the placement of *Let's Hear It for the Deaf Man* in April 1973.

[8]In *Heat* (130) we are told that Meyer had been shot in the leg "last Christmas," a reference to the episode in *Ghosts*. The point here is that *Heat* can not be dated the year after *Ghosts* because the dates I have cited will not fit the real-world calendar. Consequently, the dating in Appendix E places *Ghosts* in December 1978 and *Heat* in August 1980, both consistent with the calendar dates given in the novels.

[9]Carella's apparently faulty memory, which seems to be four years off in reference to the age of his children and the marriage of his sister, is actually not too bad as long as he does not try to compare events on different time-tracks. Bert Kling has a much worse memory for dates; he is almost always off by at least a year, and sometimes two or three. Cotton Hawes's memory is more accurate than Kling's, though he is guilty of the quite unpardonable blunder explained below in Note 2 on Chapter 10. Meyer Meyer has a good memory for dates and so (to give the devil his due) has Andy Parker. Curiously, nobody in the series ever *over*-estimates the time elapsed since some past event; it is always later than they think.

Chapter 4

[1]*Form and Ideology in Crime Fiction* (Bloomington: Indiana University

Press, 1980), p. 183.

[2]Hillary Waugh, "The Police Procedural," in *The Mystery Story,* ed. John Ball (Del Mar: University of California-San Diego, 1976), p. 174.

[3]Bill Knox, *Who Shot the Bull?* (New York: Doubleday, 1970), pp. 72-3.

[4]*The Police Procedural* (Bowling Green, Ohio: The Popular Press, 1982), pp. 125-8.

[5]*Form and Ideology in Crime Fiction,* pp. 182-3.

Chapter 5

[1]This one is in *Hail, Hail, the Gang's All Here!* The others show up in *"J",* *Like Love,* and *Blood Relatives.*

[2]*Fuzz,* 30; *Hail, Hail, the Gang's All Here!,* 88; *Bread,* 135.

Chapter 6

[1]John L. Breen, "The Jury Box," *Ellery Queen's Mystery Magazine,* August 1982, p. 82.

[2]See Appendix F. Throughout this chapter, I have used such broad categories as "murder," "assault," and "theft" without reference to the more specific kinds and degrees of these crimes. Under the heading of *murder* I am including any instance in which one person intentionally kills another. *Assault* encompasses all cases of physical attack for the purpose of inflicting injury, which would include threats with a dangerous weapon and attempted murder. *Theft* encompasses all instances in which a person steals something, and includes burglary, larceny, and fraud.

[3]Department of Justice, *Crime in the United States, 1980* (Washington, D.C.: Government Printing Office, 1981), 118. Here and subsequently, wherever I have compared a situation in real-life crime with a corresponding one from the 87th Precinct, it should be kept in mind that the factual data represent the year 1980 only, while the fictional ones cover a span from 1956 to 1983.

[4]For comparison with real life, cf. *Crime in U.S.,* p. 13: "Whites comprised 51 per cent of the total arrestees for murder in 1980. Blacks made up 48 per cent; and the remainder were of other races."

[5]*Crime in U.S.,* p. 11.

[6]*The Gentle Art of Murder* (Bowling Green: The Popular Press, 1980), p. 127.

[7]*Crime in U.S.* has a tabulation of murder motives (p. 13), but the organization is such that it is impossible to match those categories with the ones developed in the stories. My count of murders committed by persons of unsound mind is two from *"J",* and one each from *He Who Hesitates, Hail, Hail, the Gang's All Here!, Blood Relatives,* and *Calypso.*

[8]*Crime in U.S.,* p. 13.

[9]*Crime in U.S.,* p. 11.

[10]*Crime in U.S.,* p. 12.

[11]There are a few scattered cases in which there is a link between the victim's occupation and the motive for murder, as with the two city officials in *Fuzz* and Hester Mathiesen, the blind beggar in *Long Time No See,* but these are almost entirely fortuitous.

[12]*Let's Hear It for the Deaf Man,* pp. 26-7. Statistics from real life agree, at least for aggravated assault (*Crime in U.S.,* p. 21).

[13]In *Killer's Wedge.*

[14]For comparison, cf. *Crime in U.S.,* p. 21, where the per cent of distribution is as follows: Firearms, 23.9; Knife, etc., 22.0; Club, poison, etc., 27.5; Personal weapons, 26.6.

[15]Two cases involving attempted rape are counted elsewhere: the one in *Eighty Million Eyes* as assault, and the one in *So Long As You Both Shall Live* as abduction.

[16]*Crime in U.S.,* p. 118.

[17]In *The Art of the Mystery Story,* ed. Howard Haycraft (New York: Bilbo and Tannen, 1976), p. 190.

Chapter 7

[1]McBain, "The 87th Precinct," p. 91.

[2]McBain, "The 87th Precinct," p. 97.

[3]"Let him come down," says Carella, and adds, "Second Murderer, Macbeth, Act III, scene 3" (*Eighty Million Eyes,* 172). Actually, in *Macbeth,* Act III, scene 3, the *First* Murderer, in reply to Banquo's "It will rain tonight," says "Let *it* come down." The line seems to have a special tenacity; McBain's Matthew Hope recalls it (and gets it right) in *The Beauty and the Beast,* Chapter 10.

Chapter 8

[1]"Of Time and the River Harb," p. 4.

Chapter 10

[1]*He Who Hesitates,* 147-57.

[2]It is distressing that Hawes, whose memory is usually accurate, has forgotten when he met Christine. In *Bread* he remembers the meeting as "many years ago while investigating a multiple murder in a bookshop" (14), confusing the events of *Lady, Lady, I Did It!* with those of *Lady Killer.* Evidently the only association that has stuck in Hawes's mind is that of the bookshop Christine was managing at the time he met her.

Chapter 11

[1]P. 92.

[2]P. 93.

Chapter 12

[1]One exception is the place in *Give the Boys a Great Big Hand* (26-9), where he chews out Genero; the other is in *The Heckler* (68-70), where he asks Hernandez's help on a problem with a Puerto Rican youth.

Chapter 13

[1]*Form and Ideology in Crime Fiction,* pp. 191-2.

[2]"The 87th Precinct," p. 93.

Chapter 14

[1]Review of *Let's Hear It For the Deaf Man, New York Times Book Review,*
April 1, 1973, p. 34.
[2]*Anatomy of Criticism* (Princeton: Princeton University Press, 1957), p. 47.
[3]*Form and Ideology in Crime Fiction,* p. 177.
[4]George N. Dove, *The Police Procedural,* pp. 134-5.
[5]*The Police Procedural,* p. 136.
[6]Like "hand" in *Give the Boys a Great Big Hand,* "doll" in *Doll,* "blood" in
Blood Relatives, "calypso" in *Calypso.*

Chapter 15

[1]For example, George Grella, "The Hard-Boiled Detective Novel," in
Detective Fiction, ed. Robin Winks (Englewood Cliffs, N.J.: Prentice-Hall,
1980), p. 113; Carl Hoffman, "Spenser: The Illusion of Knighthood," *The
Armchair Detective* 16 (1983), 143.

Index

166